# The
# Mortician's Apprentice

What you never knew about what happens
behind the Mortuary Doors . . . . AND MORE!

by

Dr. Richard L. Perez, Ed.D.

A journey into the mysterious world of Thanatology

Printed by Create Space: an Amazon Company

ISBN:9781484994030

Disclaimer: As with all professions, there are changes that occur over the years.  This book is but a snapshot of various mortuary and autopsy lab procedures and may not include up-to-date changes that have occurred over the years since the experiences described in the book occurred.

For example, there is now no way an unlicensed person can be allowed in the prep room.

Cover page designed by Joe Hunt of
        Joe Hunt Design and Photography
        1164 Bishop Street
        Suite 124
        Honolulu, HI  96813
        www.joehunt.com

<u>Acknowledgements</u>

Great appreciation is given to my great proofreaders:

    Terry Joyce, Julia Joyce, Tom Bratton and Lynda Perez

# The Mortician's Apprentice

What you never knew about what happens
behind the mortuary doors . . . . AND MORE!

Introduction . . . . . . . . . . . . . . . . . . . . . . . . . . . . . . . . . . i-iii

Chapter 1   My Introduction to Thanatology . . . . . . . . . 1

Chapter 2   The Early Years . . . . . . . . . . . . . . . . . 20

Chapter 3   What is Forensics? . . . . . . . . . . . . . . . . 31
                 The Autopsy . . . . . . . . . . . . . . . . . 34
                      Clinical Autopsy. . . . . . . . . . . . . . 36
                      Forensic Autopsy. . . . . . . . . . . . . 39

Chapter 4   Disposition Methods . . . . . . . . . . . . . . . 46

Chapter 5   Religious/Cultural Considerations . . . . . . . . 54

Chapter 6   A New Mortuary School . . . . . . . . . . . . . . 58

Chapter 7   Mortuary Humor . . . . . . . . . . . . . . . . . 73

Epilogue . . . . . . . . . . . . . . . . . . . . . . . . . . . . . . . . 91

Glossary . . . . . . . . . . . . . . . . . . . . . . . . . . . . . . . . 94

# The Mortician's Apprentice

**What You Never Knew About what Happens behind Closed Doors**
**. . . . and more**

# Introduction

Have you ever contemplated your death?  Of course, we have all pondered the possibility of a hereafter and tried to conceive of ourselves in that "next" world.  That is, of course, if you believe in a hereafter.  Someone once said that a dead atheist is a person who is all dressed up with nowhere to go.  If we ponder the future of our souls, some will have a happy feeling about the life after death (a circular theory) and others will consider that the lights merely go out (a linear theory where the totality of life is from A (birth) to B (death) and no further.

I grew up with a fascination with the human body and how it works.  I also wondered what would happen to my remains after death and I had questions about what will they do with my body?  <u>What really goes on beyond those closed doors at the mortuary and the Autopsy room?</u>  How will they dispose of me?  Should I be afraid of death and all the circumstances that surround it?  Will I sense anything in my personal subconscious?  The questions seemed interminable.

My interest in this began at a very early age.  I was an altar boy in my church and served at many funerals.  I was satisfied with the idea of my passing, but, I felt certain that, as a God-fearing individual, I would pass on to an eternal life.  I realized that my body was merely a carcass which was enlivened only by the presence of a God-given soul.  I knew that at death, the body and soul would be headed in different directions.  I knew that the soul would be cared for in my eternal life, but, how will they dispose of my carcass?

As a young person, I pondered those questions which seemed to arise frequently during my life experiences.  I was only 8 years of age when I experienced my first opportunity to enter into the world of death exploration. While my peers cowered at the thought of such eerie concerns, I became seriously interested in it and I was dead set (sic) to embrace the study of it as I grew older..  In addition to that, I developed a talent for art and I thought it would be 'neat' to learn to draw intricate things.  I started with old broken-down buildings (like from the old west), gnarly trees and junk piles.  One day, I found an illustration of a skeleton and muscles

i

on it. I tried to emulate that drawing and, to my pleasant surprise, it came out pretty well. From that point onward, I made additional anatomical drawings and began to draw (like Netter) as much as I could. Because of my natural interest in anatomical art and my interest in death, I developed a penchant toward both in my early life. I searched for a way to combine them.

I was always fascinated with the structures and functions of the human body - and especially the miracle of its creation. This book is a peek into my early years and how I became not only interested, but, involved in the 'death business.' I didn't know it at the time, but, I was entering the world of 'thanatology.' (Gr. a study of the phenomena of death and coping). I studied the Egyptian mummies and the Egyptian process of embalming to prepare dead human beings for disposal. It is from that origin that we have developed the modern process of embalming. The vital role of the Nile River was prominent because of its provision of water for the region and had an effect on the procedures regarding the handing death. As a result, the Egyptians conducted funerals that lasted over 1000 days; it meant that embalming, therefore, had to be very thorough. They had learned that the decay of an unembalmed buried body in the sandy soil eventually liquified and caused a detrimental affect on the water table - increases in illnesses, for example. The embalming was invented as a way to assure that water remained safe to drink.

The processes of handling death can be viewed from at least three sides;
    1) from the standpoint of the family as they deal with bereavement
    2) from the standpoint of one's own thoughts and considerations about death
    3) from the standpoint of those who have entered into a career of service to the families of  bereaved.

This book is an insight to the business of death and one man's travels through the many aspects of working with death and body disposal. It explores the processes and decision-making areas which are fraught with many choices that go into taking care of someone who has died and the need to serve the surviving family members with dignified and professional services. There will be much more to be said after this as technology improves and as burial land dwindles. This is an overview (with some detail) of the concerns the general public might have about <u>what happens behind those closed doors.</u>

Historically, the death and disposal of a loved one was a private family matter. At first, body preparation was done in the home and burial was, more than often, in the family back yard.  Many of the homes had parlors where a deceased person could be viewed by family and friends.  With the advent of funeral homes, the viewing began to take place in the Mortuary parlor.  From then on, our former home parlors were renamed "living rooms."

There are many fascinating aspects to the business of death resolution.  I hope to allay one's fears about the subject of death.  Of course, death is a serious matter and the approach to taking care of the dead is a very serious business.  In fact, most people cringe when faced with conversation with a funeral director or pathologist.  They may be hesitant to make conversation without reference to that type of person's profession or, they may feel a great fascination that anyone would make a career choice to get involved in the death business.  It may seem impossible, but there have been many moments of humor among the personnel who do such work.  Every mortician has a story or two about something humorous that happened during their watches.  Some have been included here.

I hope your future contacts with the world of death and the activities that surround it will be more appreciated after you have read this book.  It is my hope that you will develop a different view of death and come to appreciate the challenge that awaits anyone who would aspire to working in such an environment.  I know that you will learn the scope of the job of the mortician and be able to get around statements such as - "Well, someone has to do it!" when referring to his work.  Such workers operate in a clean and safe workplace and work closely with people who are in mourning (grief).  The work has many scientific facets and is gaining more respect from professionals in the medical community.

This book is a serious approach to explore and explain the job of mortician and the challenges he faces every day.  His knowledge of anatomy, chemistry and thanatochemistry, business and accounting, restorative art and cosmetizing, marketing and management, purchasing and merchandising, computer use, counseling, mortuary law and embalming is extensive.  It is all meant to provide professional services for families.

Times have changed and more modernization has occurred.  There have been many procedural changes and improvements which have taken place since my work in the thanatology business ended.  The mortuary schooling has tried to keep with the profession so as to produce well-trained professional men and women to serve as embalmers and funeral directors.

# 1

## My Introduction to Thanatology*

*(From the Greek - Thanatos - study of the phenomenon of death)

It was a long time ago, in a far away small town when I met up with the concept of death. I had not yet experienced the loss of anyone in my family, nor had I been present in any situations wherein a death had occurred. It was a word we used as children as we played cowboys or alien fighters. We knew that when you said, "Bang, you're dead!" that that was the end of that fight, but, that we could get up and fight again. We went to movie matinees where, death was seen regularly in Westerns, Gangster Films, Monster shows or, especially in movies which featured our favorite super heroes. We even noted that some actors were killed in one movie, then appeared in another one. As we grew older, we frequently watched movies which featured death and, perhaps, began to develop a skewed view of it.

So, boys, grew to accept death as a form of entertainment and came to recognize that those things happened to the "bad guys" or to soldiers (good guys) in movies. As a result, the concept of death took its place in our imaginations and was applied it only to movies and occasional stories in the news. We witnessed the death and resurgence of many famous persons as they appeared in different movies. We were always bystanders from far away and it was movie-death taught us to dismiss death as a reality from our personal subconscious. In church, we have learned that death was another phase of our existence which followed and it led our inner conscientious understanding of the life we are living. In the end, we either treated the subject with ignorance or with a lack of fear because of the afterlife we had not come to understand it. We came to realize that people had developed different understandings of death and its aftermath. Some felt that when life ended, it represented the end of a linear lifecycle, i.e. there was no afterlife. Other people considered death as apart of the lifecycle - as a cyclical process where the end of one phase (life) ended, but then, continued because of its circular nature.

The cyclical view seemed to be more positive to us - after all, our comic book and movie heroes went on to live continual lives. In essence it appeared that one's concept of life and death depended upon one's world view and his relationship to a spiritual understanding of life after death. That was, of course, too complicated for a kid to contemplate. I guess that, in my case, it was a question which remained in my mind as I began to question aspects of and inquired about the death and dying process.

When I was confronted with the death of someone I had known, I began to ask more questions. What was it that went on behind the closed doors of the mortuary? As a result of my curiosity, my quest for further information seemed to grow and my fascination with the death process continued. Some people, on the other hand, perhaps most, have developed a great fear of death.

As an 8 year-old cub scout; it was not a problem when I joined a den of scouts and learned that the scout leader was the town mortician and our funeral director and that the meetings were to be held at his mortuary. For us boys, it was sort-of exciting - it was not so with our parents as they were "spooked" at the mere sound of funeral home, or mortuary. They were even hesitant to allow us to go to that place. In the end, they had an adult take us to the scout meetings. It was usually one of my uncles who was assigned that dreadful duty.

Life as an 8 year-old cub scout in a mortuary was quite an undertaking (sic). We met in an old stately mansion-like three-story home with columns and attics and dormers with windows which had fancy wooden trim on them. Of course, it had the expected spider webs in the right places and had a very eerie look - especially under a bright moonlit sky. It was very much like some we have seen in the comic books we had been reading. It was perfect for setting up a haunted house for Halloween. It was very eerie to drive by at night when you could see a dim light beaming from one window late into the evening. Most people, on foot, would cross the street to pass it on the other side. Not many people realized that a family actually resided within its walls. One of them, another 8 year old boy, was my friend who was also a member of my scout den.

His name was Charlie; he and I were friends at school. I never had realized that Charlie was the son of the local mortician. Boy! Did I have a head full of questions for him?

Our scout meetings were held near the main entrance to a great hallway. We met in a small alcove-type of room next to a large parlor room where they held visitations and funerals. The entry was very large and ornate. There were small rooms completely around the perimeter. The room where we met was one of them, but it was larger than the others. There was an even large parlor; it was a room with ancient roots; parlor referred to a private reception room such as this which was

2

customarily used for other types of businesses, i.e. beauty parlor, funeral parlor. At one time, it may have been called the 'locutorium,' such as those found in a monastery. Many private homes of the past had an entry room which was also called the parlor. At times, it served as a place where a family could hold a family visitation where the member's body could 'lie in state' in the home where the deceased had lived. When that practice ended, that room became known as a "living" room. The mortuary also had several smaller rooms called 'slumber rooms' where families could visit privately with their loved ones who were lying in state in a coffin or it could be made up to simulate a bedroom where the deceased could look natural in a normal bed.

At first, it seemed that this meeting place would be somewhat spooky. What if we were left alone in our meeting room as we waited for our leader? I guess I would be comfortable because I was assured that I would never be left alone in there and I would usually be surrounded by other people my age and, perhaps, at least one adult. If I were to be there alone, I am sure my feelings would be different – I might just take off and run home. Actually, it was a moment I readily cherished. I was curious and wanted to take advantage of any downtime we could find to explore the house. Of course, we were more fearful of being caught than anything else. I leaned on my friend, Charlie, who resided in the house with his family; his father was the mortician.

In actuality though, Charlie, himself, had not seen certain parts of the house; he had been restricted from entering certain areas. We both had had a great deal of curiosity In our desire to explore the house. We would have to watch our time, since, it was a very large house and we had to search it in short segments of time so as not to be found missing at any time from the meeting room. So, over time, we expected to explore a great amount of the house in small areas or segments based upon the amount of time we had available to ourselves.

The day finally arrived when we were to have our first cub scout meeting at the mortuary. I had to remind my parents about it, since they preferred to forget about it. I had spoken with Charlie at school and he was anxious to have me come to his house. The time arrived for me to get ready to go; I donned my cub scout uniform then I encouraged my uncle, who was at home, to take me to the meeting and pick me up afterward. He had a rickety old truck, which would embarrass me in the daylight. Since it was evening and getting darker, it was easier for me to be OK about driving up to this mansion-looking building in such a vehicle. The driveway usually had Cadillac limos parked in the circular driveway.

As we approached the house, it shown in a stately manner as a large silhouette against a darkening sky. It was lit up; the porch was especially well-lit and shining brightly. The truck chugged in and parked in front of the main entrance with very ornate molding in an overhang which surrounded the entire front and side porches. My uncle let me off and I scampered up the stairway to the main entrance. It felt as if I were entering a mansion. I waved to my uncle as he drove off. I think I felt like an ancient knight arriving at my castle after a hard day of fighting off the enemy.

Charlie met me and we entered into a grand room with chandeliers and fancy trim everywhere. There was a grand wide swooping carpeted staircase which led up to the second floor. All of the wood rails were carved and fancy. Charlie greeted me and led me to the room beside the staircase where our scout meeting would be held. I was the first one to arrive, so Charlie and I discussed the situation and made plans for our first excursion. Before we had a chance to begin our trip, another scout arrived. His name was David; Charlie led him to the meeting room where we could all wait for the meeting to begin.

On our first excursion in the house, Charlie and I edged our way to an adjacent room; the door was closed so we edged up to it and placed our ears on the keyhole to make certain that no one was in there- especially the mortician himself. We eased the door open. The creaking scared us so we tried to open it very slowly. We stopped and checked the area to make certain that we had not been heard. Finally, the door was open enough for us to sidle in to one side of the room. We closed the door and crouched near the wall and we worried that our heavy breathing, which might be heard by someone in the house. It was fairly dark, but we could see a little because of the light, which emanated from the large entryway which was well-lit; there was also some light from the room we had just left. We didn't want to turn on a major light for fear that we would be found out. Charlie said that this was the casket room (sometimes called the Display Room), which was full of different types of caskets. David told us that they were arranged according the value of each one. The most expensive one was up front and then worked back to the least expensive. This was the place where people would come in to select a casket or burial urn for a funeral. Most of the caskets were on biers (a frame or stand with wheels upon which a coffin was set).  The roller wheels allowed for easy movement.  These were used to hold a casket with a corpse inside in order to be able to roll it into the chapel or outside to the hearse (a vehicle which is a specially designed car or carriage designed for transporting bodies);  it was also used to carry a coffin, (casket) to a place of worship in a church, to the cemetery or crematorium) and then, ultimately, to the gravesite.

I found out, the hard way, just how mobile such a device the bier was when I tried to lean on an open casket and my weight pushed the entire unit and it rolled away from me.  It nearly hit another casket which was on another bier.  Charlie helped me to stop rolling, since I could have caused a domino effect; that would have been a real disaster!  By then, it was time to return to our meeting room, but also, because we just had a close call.  It was fortunate that we had avoided a serious catastrophe in the casket room - what if the Mahogany casket had been marred?.  It was difficult to stop shaking after our little adventure, but we did manage to join our scout meeting and eventually participate normally.  Charlie and I chuckled at each other as we recollected our recent experience in the casket room.

That was our first exploration and we were so excited; we could hardly wait to come back for another search of the mortuary house.  We had a natural curiosity about a lot of things in general, but especially, about the mortuary.  The spooky aspect of our excursions was secondary to the fun we were having.

On our next meeting night at the mortuary, we tried to arrive earlier than before so we could have more time to explore.  On this occasion, our new friend, David, joined us and we wanted to take him into the casket room.  We had told him that we had explored it; we didn't mention anything about the close call we had had with the rolling casket.  When the coast was clear, we retraced our previous steps, Charlie opened the door and we entered as we had done the previous week.

I warned our new partner, David, about the possible movement of the biers and that too much weight could roll them into other items in the room.  (At this time, we didn't now that the bier had wheel locks).  Wow! What if we were to crash caskets into each other and cause damage?  We now could be certain that the bier wheels were locked before we started.  We realized that rolling caskets could be a near-fatal (for us) mistake.  Now, however, I wanted to take the next step and look inside a casket.  That would take at least two of us since neither of us were tall

5

enough to see inside one without help. After we locked the wheels, we devised a plan where the two of them, Charlie and David, would hold my feet and lift me high enough to see into the coffin. They set their hands to hold my feet, so, I stepped on them carefully, grabbed the top edge of the casket and pulled myself up and looked inside the casket. It was silky and frilly and had a nice pillow and the bed of it was semi-soft, but very thin; (it was filled with shredded newspaper and covered with a nice material to match the linings). I could feel the solid floor through it. When my friends became tired of holding me, they let me down.

We decided to let David try it next. He was shorter than the two of us, but, he was lighter and easier to lift. Unfortunately as we lifted him and he reached for the edge of the casket. He missed the inner ledge and caught the side rail; from that point, we began a whirlwind spin until David fell out of our hands and the casket and bier continued to spin around in the room and finally came to rest against the door we had entered. Oops! We missed one of the wheel locks and another wasn't holding. We just knew that someone had heard the slamming into the door; fortunately, however, there was no response. Our next task was to move the casket-bearing bier back to its place on the floor. We didn't realize that this casket was made of mahogany and probably heavier than any other casket in the room. As a result, it became a monumental task for the three of us to unlock the wheels and roll it back into place. After some heavy lifting, maneuvering and severe sweating, we succeeded. We locked the wheels again and hurried back through the door and took our places in the meeting room - just in time - as the leader was arriving. He looked at us mysteriously and wondered why we were so flush and sweaty. Charlie told him that we had been running in the yard before he had arrived.

Time passed and we arrived for our next cub scout meeting and the three of us immediately gathered to plan our next adventure. We realized that we had to be extremely aware of our timing so as not to get caught. Charlie went to the door to make certain that the coast was clear. At his signal, we crept into the casket room once again. It was a cavernous room, but items were difficult to distinguish due to the reduced lighting. We walked around the various items, a tombstone display, a wall of urns and a very large rack of clothing. Upon reaching the last row, we noticed an open casket mounted on a slanted display rack and it was low enough for us to get a real close look inside of it. Charlie was smart enough to bring a flashlight and David wanted to climb into the casket to lie in it and "try it out." Since it was so low, the bottom edge was only knee high to us, so, David climbed in and then he asked us to close the lid; he wanted to see what it was like to be inside of it. We jiggled and poked around and finally found the release for the lid and it closed - loudly; David was now inside and pretended he was lying in repose. The lid had slammed down hard - shut! It made a tremendous noise and Charlie and I dashed to the door of the room to see if anyone else had heard it. It was a very quiet building, so, we were fortunate that we had not been detected in that room. As we returned to the casket where David was inside, we heard the thumping and kicking and muffled cries as he tried to open the lid. We called to him (in whispered tones); (unfortunately, he couldn't hear us) and tried to lift the lid - but, it was to no avail. It seems that the lid has a catch-mechanism in it so that exit was nearly impossible. (It is actually possible when you realize how the latch was constructed and that it could be manipulated from the inside). David was entering a full-panic state; we continued to look for a way to open the lid. He finally calmed down when he realized that we there working on it.

I always wondered, why it should lock down, and why anyone should be able to open it FROM THE INSIDE? It was also curious to realize that it COULD be opened from the inside. I didn't think corpses would want to be let out. (Ha Ha). After a lot of searching, we found the release latch (outside, under the lip of the lid), so, Charlie and I released the latch. We worked to lift the heavy lid (it was especially heavy since the casket it was on a slanted rack) to let David out. His face was flushed and had a look of tremendous fear on it. He wanted to run home, but we held him back and tried to calm him down before we headed for the scout meeting room. We returned everything to its proper place and 'calmly' went to our meeting - although we had just had a huge scare.

The next day, I saw Charlie at school and we talked about our latest experience in the casket room. I asked him about the "jar" and small box display I had seen in that room. He said that that was a burial urn which is used by some people who do not want to be placed in a casket after they died and that they preferred cremation (a process wherein the body is burned in a retort after death and the ashes are placed in an urn). (A retort is the oven chamber wherein the body is reduced to ashes by fire - 1600 F for 5-6 hours - newer ones are faster). I asked him if many people preferred that method, he replied that in his father's funeral home that, in the past, casket burials were most favored, and lately, perhaps, more than half of the cases used cremation. Many people prefer it because of its lower cost and that long extensive services typically were not necessary. I then asked him, what happens to the urns? He said that the families usually returned to collect the urn, then, they either bury it or they (with a government permit) scatter the ashes somewhere such as in the woods or in a lake, river or ocean. He went on to say that some families don't come back to get the ashes, so, we have several cremated bodies stored in the house. In some states, the unclaimed ashes (as with bodies) are buried in County cemeteries.

At home, everything was calm. My parents asked about the scout meetings and I think they were curious about the funeral home. I told them that I was having a great time at the scout meetings, but I avoided any talk about our excursions in the mortuary building itself.

At our next cub scout meeting, the three of us gathered with great anxiety as we considered our next exploration target. Expectedly, David was a bit nervous as he reeled from his last visit inside a locked casket. We tried to ease his mind until he could calm down enough to launch out on another expedition. We thought we might take one more look into the casket room to see if there was anything we had missed. This time, we each carried a flashlight. We again moved stealthily toward the casket room door, looked around, and entered. It was beginning to look familiar now. We noticed how David, understandably, wanted to avoid the area with the low casket display. In the rear corner of the room, I noticed a rack of very nice clothes. I asked Charlie about them and he said he wasn't certain, but, it appeared to him that all the clothes were cut down the back along the seam. That seemed weird to us; we could not imagine why that was the case. I reached under a plastic bag which covered a coat and, sure enough, the back was loosely basted - it was clear that these clothes could be separated into two halves. Charlie said that he would ask his father about that. Although interesting, this was the least eventful night we had had in our mortuary explorations.

When we returned for another cub scout meeting, we wanted to consider finding another part of the mortuary. We found another adjacent room in the large entry way which had a sign on it which read, "Arrangements." As we entered the open doorway, we noticed that it looked like a typical business office. In one corner, we noticed stacks of books. They looked like catalogues and, sure enough, there were pictures of caskets, clothes, mortuary equipment such as biers and flower holders in it. We found catalogues of tombstones, mouth closers (what is that?), trocar's (tro-kar), (what is a trocar?), small stainless steel nails with wires on them (what are those?) urns, stationery, and everything a mortuary would need. Some of it was pretty weird. What were those plastic half-shells with the standing rough lifted cutouts? We didn't get scared on this trip, but we did see a lot of things in those catalogues that the mortuary may want to have on hand.  These things raised an even greater curiosity within us.

As we went to our meeting room, we were fresh and calm.  However, I had a strange curiosity about some of those things I had seen in the office in the catalogues.

At school, I continued to meet with Charlie and to ask a thousand questions.  I asked him if he was going to grow up and do what his dad does.  He said he didn't know yet.  In fact, he said, "I don't **really** know what my dad does."  I asked him if there were some other interesting escapades we could do in the mortuary.  He said that he knew of a few places he would like to show us and that he would like to explore in some areas that had been designated as taboo to him.  That sounded real exciting and I couldn't wait to go to our next cub scout meeting.

Another scout meeting time arrived and my uncle dutifully drove me to the mortuary.  I could hardly wait to exit the car as he drove into the round driveway.  It was a neat grassy and flower-trimmed driveway, since it led right up to the house and under a porch-like roof and exited the other side.  He left me off at the side door under the porch roof and I met Charlie as I entered the house.  I told him that I really liked his house - it was so big.  He laughed and said he thought it was **too** big.  I asked him about the large black limousine that was parked in the back yard.  He said that that was just one of the big cars they had - there were five more in the garage back there too.  I was amazed; I had never seen such a large garage. I asked him if we could get a closer look at the car.  He agreed to take me out to the car where we could inspect it more closely.  It was an extra-large black station-wagon-looking car - I asked, "Is a hearse!"  He said, "No, this is called a Family Car.  It is a large sedan used to transport the immediate family members to the church and to the cemetery."  When we arrived at the car, we found that it was locked.  We were disappointed, but then, he said he thought we could get into a car in the garage to see another one.  That sounded like a good plan, so, we went around to the back of the garage and entered a door.

Once inside, we noticed a row of long black cars.  One as a hearse and the others were large (stretched) four-door sedans (family cars).  There were not many windows in the building.  I noted to David that we were in a dark place again trying to see things.  David agreed.  We proceeded toward the hearse, checked, and it was open.  As we got prepared to get into the car, David said that they did not refer to these cars as **hearses** any more; it was more proper now to call them *"funeral coaches."* I guess that reduced some of the morbidity associated with it. We climbed into the driver's seat and we could see all the controls and the hand radio the driver could use during a funeral procession (that was strange). The hearse also had radio. That seemed strange to me; it made me wondered about that. He said that during a funeral, the driver could listen to music as he "made it through all the lights" - after all, he was escorted by police through all the traffic lights at the intersections - he never had to stop. The only problem is that in a Cadillac, when you turned the radio on, the antenna goes up. I asked him if it would be possible for me to ride a car like this in a funeral procession. He told me that it was not probable - he had never even done it himself.

The seats were very plush and looked hardly used. Charlie told me that these cars are very sturdy and since they were only used at funerals, and since they were replaced every two years or so, they typically had very low mileage - they would be great used cars! I wondered, who would want to own a private hearse? We opened the window which separated the front seat from the rear section; we were able to crawl through it into a huge flat space at the rear; it had ridged rails embedded in the floor. This was where a casket was carried to the cemetery. I don't know why, but I sensed a strange odor within this part of the car. Perhaps, this was the reason for the window behind the driver. "No," Charlie said, "that was merely the odor of the disinfectant they used to clean the car after each service."

He took me around to the rear of the hearse, opened the door. He moved a cover that disclosed a series of buttons. When he pressed one and the large floor of the hearse began to roll out. We didn't have enough space for it to rollout completely, so, he stopped it right away and returned it to its starting position. It was very interesting to see the inside of a hearse. He had another surprise as he moved to the side of the hearse and opened a side door. He found another set of buttons and when he pressed one, the floor began to spin around and it turned to slide sideways as we sat on it; it turned until the end of it protruded out of the side of the car. (We had plenty of space on the side). He said that there were times when the "side-loader" was more convenient for unloading a casket at a cemetery or at a church. After that neat experience, we walked back to the house to begin our cub scout meeting.

At school, I met Charlie and told him how much I had enjoyed inspecting the hearse at his mortuary. I told him I couldn't wait to grow up and be able to drive one. He told me that he enjoyed our little excursion too, but that, he was anxious about seeing more rooms in the house.

The time had come when another cub scout meeting was to be held. As it turned out, the meeting had been cancelled since the mortician (our scout leader) was going to be out of town. What a shock! (ha-ha). To me it sounded like an opportunity! I called Charlie to ask him about it and he was disappointed too, since he was having such fun showing David and me around the mortuary. I agreed that this was a bummer, since I was enjoying the exploration so much. He then said, " I have an idea!" "Why don't you come over anyway - we can do our homework together and then I can show you more stuff." "Since my dad is away, we can have more freedom to explore." I said, "What a great idea, I was thinking about that, but I will have to get my parents to let me go there." We said goodbye and I pondered how I was going to get my parents to let me go the mortuary when the scout meeting had been cancelled. But wait! They didn't know about the cancellation.

When my father came home from work, he was extremely tired and wanted to go to bed right after supper. I thought, "Great! That's one down." I knew that mom would be a hard sell, since she really didn't like for me to go there - even for scout meetings. I told her that Charlie and I were working on a school project and that I need to meet with him early to work on it. At first, she was totally against it. I told her that I could go on my bike - she said "Absolutely Not!" I figured that that was it, so I began to mope and wish that I could have gone over there to see Charlie. Luckily, my uncle walked in and said that he was going out for a little while, so, I asked him if he could take me to Charlie's house (notice, I didn't mention the Mortuary) and pick me up on his way home. He said he could, so, after some more negotiating with my mom, I jumped into the car with my uncle and he took me to Charlie's house.

When I arrived at the mortuary, Charlie was outside ready to greet me. I told him how I had come close of missing out on this meeting. We started to go into the side door, but, he said wait, "Let's go into the basement." Now that was a scary thought, but he said that his dad was out of town and his mother was working in the kitchen; he said that it would be all right and, since he had never been in there, he thought it could be exciting. In fact, he thought it would be better since the house was so large, it would be very difficult to detect our presence - especially in the basement.

He led me to a rear entrance, which was directly under the kitchen and we had to move very quickly and quietly into the entrance. He opened the creaky door into a large dark entryway where the stairs began an immediate downward slope. We went down a couple of steps, closed the door and turned on a light, briefly. We gathered our bearings and Charlie showed me his flashlight, turned off the light and we began to move into a dark room. At the bottom of the stairs, he turned on his flashlight again and we found a large open space. It looked like what I had imagined as an old time laboratory room. It had tables and tanks and drawers and hoses all around. It looked like a hospital laboratory room. In an adjacent room, we found a room full of gurneys (hospital-type tables used for carrying bodies). On one of them was a covered figure, which was probably a human body. Wow, this was my chance to see an actual dead body. We edged up to it and dared each other to uncover it - neither of us was that brave, so we decided to do it together on the count of three. At the count of three, we pulled back the cover, cowered and fell to the ground. When we stood up, slowly, we were surprised to see that we had uncovered a CPR dummy. After we regained our composure, we roared with laughter (quietly) at our trepidations and actions.

We returned to the first room; we thought it would be neat to investigate the bottles of liquid; the counter was covered with stainless steel tools and instruments. In the center, was another gurney-like table (but, a bit larger), which had troughs on both sides and had an opening at the bottom - like a drain. We began to think that this was the actual workroom for a person such as a scientist might use. It looked like a real laboratory filled with glass tubes and containers. In another room, we found more gurneys with more figures on them. We chuckled and thought this must be a storage place for CPR dummies. I confidently strode forth and pulled a cover from the first table and was shocked to see that this was a dead human being. "Yikes!" What have we found? When we turned around, we noticed that the door had a sign which said "holding room" and another one with an arrow pointing to the larger room we had seen with the tanks and the main table, the sign read "Prep Room." We had just found a room with, at least, five dead bodies in it.

Then it happened, we heard the outer door creak open and then footsteps coming down the stairs into the basement. We hid in the holding room behind some gurneys and cowered down in the corner behind the sheet, which was draped over the gurney. Had Charlie's father returned home from his trip? We heard the person rattling some instruments and we could hear various noises. We moved quietly to where we could see through a narrow slit in the door, which was slightly ajar. We then scampered back to our hiding place. We saw a figure wrapped in a smock, an apron, a mask, a surgical hat and rubber gloves walking into the room where we were hiding. The figure had only a small slit in his mask, which allowed him to see where he was going. As he entered the room, he began inspecting "toe tags" (these are used in morgues to identify bodies). He selected one which, was only two tables away from where we were hiding; (I was certain that someone could have heard my teeth chattering with fear) he pulled it out and rolled it next to the main table in the large lab-type room. We heard grunting and straining as the body was moved from the gurney onto the main table. The gurney was washed down and returned to the room where we had been hiding. I am certain that we had not taken a breath during that time we were hiding in that room. It was a very close call! We were visibly shaking as we decided to make our way quietly to the door of the holding room. From that position, we could see the activity in that lab-type room.

The man in the smock and mask was turned toward the counter (away from us), so, we contemplated sneaking out and running up the stairs and outside. Charlie said that would be too noisy and the man would surely recognize us, report us and have us punished. Instead, we crept closer to the table and settled in to a cozy place behind some boxes and storage items from which we could watch the proceedings. I believe that this body was about to get embalmed. (treatment of a dead body to preserve it with chemicals, drugs or balsams).

The body was first washed down thoroughly and towel-dried. The operator placed folded towels over the face and the abdomen of the body. He then moved to another counter at the head of the main table and poured some pink liquid into a glass tank with a scale of measurements printed on the side. That only filled the tank about 1/5th of the way - he then added water to fill the tank. It now had a nice pinkish milky tone of appearance. He then added another liquid, which was dark in color and that reduced the pink look of the mixture to a darker pink tone. That was a dye, which is used to stain the original pink liquid - without the dye, the body would never assume a natural color appearance - it would be too light. After the tank was ready, he adjusted a dial on the tank - with the motor turned off, he left it at 20. (Later, I found that that represented 20 pounds of pressure).

He left the tank there ready to run. He then emerged with a scalpel in his hand and stood above the right shoulder of the body. This was bad for us, since he partially obscured our view of the procedure. We tried to shift without causing any noise.

13

Charlie said that he could see a little better and he whispered to me what he could see. When the operator moved to the other side of the table, I was able to see better. The operator located a spot on the neck near the collar bone and made a small incision. He then used two instruments which looked like scalpel blade handles without blades) but with L-shaped tips. He appeared to dig into the body slightly until he pulled up a blood vessel. It was shiny and he trimmed and separated the outer sheath. He then placed two ligatures (cord ties) with long ends about 3 or 4 inches apart. He secured them tightly, then cut the vessel in between the ties and used the long ends to restrain the ends from withdrawing into the body. He then placed a cannula (an angular metal tube) and inserted it into the end of the cut vessel. The long ends of the string are loosened slightly in order to allow the cannula to enter freely. The cannula is ridged and the tie is replaced to connect it securely. The end of the cannula has a hose, which is directly connected to the glass machine with the pink liquid. At that point, the machine is turned on and begins to pump the 20 pounds of pressured darkened pink liquid into the lower right carotid artery which supplies circulation to join the Aorta so that the normal circulation route of the blood as it moves through the heart and to the other parts of the body and all of its extremities.

As the fluid is pumped in, I wondered what happened to the blood that was already in the body. The operator loosened the other end of the artery which was being held with the long-ended strings. Immediately, blood began to flow out of that end onto the table and down to the drain. The operator waited until the color changed from dark red to the pink color of the liquid being pumped. When that happened, he knew that the flow was done and that he can complete that phase. The fluid was being pushed into the body and, in turn, pushed out the remaining blood in the body. This demonstrated what is meant by a 'closed system;' the natural flow of the circulatory system is used to assure that all the vessels, down to the capillaries receive the embalming fluid. I noticed that the operator massaged the fingers to assure that the tips of the fingers were receiving fluid.

He turned off the machine and removed the cannula making certain that his strings were still available to shut off the flow or back-flow in the artery. He then inserted the cannula into the upper part of the carotid artery (at the neck) which was cut initially. He reset the machine to 3-5 pounds of pressure. He then clipped the jugular vein slightly; this allows the blood from the head to drain without affecting the rest of the body. He massaged the face and, after a few minutes, the drained fluid cleared and the head was finished. He removed the cannula, tightened the

14

ligature, added one to the jugular vein and the embalming process was complete.

Although the embalming process was completed, the full body preparation was not. The embalmer tucked the ligatured vessels back under the skin and began to sew the wound. This takes great skill since you don't want an ugly scar to show at the funeral. It is interesting to note that this wound location is typical for male bodies, while for female bodies, the embalming entrance incision is usually at the femoral artery (on the thigh). Since women may be expected to wear clothing (in the casket), which is more revealing of the neck, the femoral placement of the incision is better.

After the incision was completed, the operator moved to the face. (Some embalmers prefer to begin with the face, since men require shaving - he shaved him and closed the eyes and secured them by inserting small plastic caps with "v-cut" slits to hold the eyelids down; (So that is how those things we had seen in the catalogue were used). For some embalmers, they may prefer to begin with the face so, after the mouth and eyes were completed, they would (normally) proceed to the embalming process (just described). In this case, however, that had already been done. After this person was shaved, the operator manipulated the jaw to make certain that he could establish a clean and natural position of the bite. He then retrieved this hideous-looking tool that looks like a steel-plated hypodermic syringe. He inserted a small nail which had a wire attached, (So that is what those things were in the catalogue), and, essentially, stapled the nail into the upper gum. He then reloaded the instrument and shot another staple into the lower gum. He then had two long wires emerging from the gums which he tied together assuring that the teeth were closing naturally. He then used cream on the lips and positioned them with his fingers (like a fine sculptor) for a natural look. The eyes and lips may receive a little super glue at final cosmetizing (farding).

It appeared that the process was essentially over, but then the operator grabbed a long chrome tubular steel rod with a hose connected to it which was connected to the large tank of fluid. He replaced the cannula with the end of the chrome tube. It had a large point and he proceeded to insert the rod into the abdomen of the body (near the navel), turned on the machine again and moved the rod from side to side in a sort-of fan-like pattern inside the abdomen as it pumped fluid into the body. It was also meant to aspirate any gases which may be present. Wow, that was interesting!

When he had completed that task, he sealed the opening with a plastic button and the operator began to remove his protective clothing, i.e. the surgical cap - WHAT? Long hair fell from the cap; the gloves, the apron and the mask were then removed. At that point, we nearly screamed with surprise (and fear, I guess) - the person who had been doing all these things to that dead body was CHARLIE'S MOM! We thought she was upstairs in the kitchen. We gasped and tried mightily not to move or make a sound, but we could barely hold it. She covered the body and rolled it to the holding room. While she was in there, the coast was clear, so we scampered up the stairway and ran out of the building. Charlie was as white as a ghost to realize that his mother was an embalmer! We were lucky that we were not seen and caught - what could we have said?

It was raining outside and the sky was very dim and cloudy. We ran to the garage for shelter. As we entered noisily, we found one of the automobile mechanics was inside working on an engine; he noticed our sense of urgency and asked us what we were doing. We told him that we were just playing outside and that we came in for shelter from the rain.

We moved closer to where he was working and he very kindly explained all the work he was doing to the car. By then, our nervousness had abated and we began to focus on the work that was being done on the car. After about an hour, we decided to call it a day. We thanked the mechanic, parted and told each other what fun we had had and that we looked forward to another adventure in the Mortuary. About that time, my uncle drove up and I jumped in with him for the ride home.

Scout meeting night arrived again and I met Charlie and David at the mortuary. We snickered about what we had seen last week and David wondered what we had done (especially since we felt as if our hearts had almost stopped!). We told him that Charlie and I had met last week and that we had had a good time. We didn't want to reveal what we had seen, but, we told him that we had had a v-e-r-y interesting time. We wanted us to tell him all about it, but we deflected him toward our next adventure for this night. We were early and we found that that allowed us more time to skulk around the house.

Charlie led the way into the basement where we again saw the hidden prep-room. David had not seen this before, so, he was slightly "spooked" by what he could see. We showed him the holding room with the bodies and he shrieked. Charlie took us through a door at the rear of that room. It appeared as if it had not been

16

opened for many years. He said he had been told not to open it. It creaked as we struggled to push it open and we moved very slowly. We all used our shoulders to push it open enough to get through it. The problem was that there was no light. Charlie went back to the prep-room to search for a light. David and I waited in the dark, but not far from the door. Suddenly, we heard the outer door open; someone entered and came down the stairs and turned on the light. We pushed the door to the holding room until it was mostly closed. What happened to Charlie? He was in that lab room. After a couple of minutes the unknown person turned off the light and went back up the stairs and the door closed. We reopened our door and waited to see if Charlie had been able to hide in time. We saw a beam from a flashlight approaching - it was Charlie and he had fortunately found a hiding place to avoid the person who had entered. (Charlie and I had a good idea who that could have been).

We were determined to see what was going on behind this newly found door. The flashlight was great as we worked our way down a hallway. We came upon another door, opened it and found another stairway going down deeper below the house. The stairs were very creaky and were mostly broken. We slowly crept down into the dark - only the flashlight allowed us to explore this area. As we reached the bottom of the stairs, we found a soft dirt floor; we could feel sunken areas - (even holes large enough to fall into). The atmosphere was very musty and spider webs were everywhere. David was very scared and wanted to stay behind, but, it was so dark, he was afraid to do that. Charlie shined the light into a corner where we spotted a number of caskets on the ground. They looked as if they had been discarded many years ago. While we had a flashlight, it was difficult to discern much detail.

The caskets were very old, broken up and covered with dust and spider webs. As we neared the first one we noticed that the cover had become deteriorated and crashed into itself. It was a very old-style casket; the lower part of it was tapered to the bottom end. Charlie said, this is what they call a "toe-pincher;" it was typical of caskets, which were used in the old west. We moved in closer and Charlie placed a light on it; he jumped back as he noticed some bones inside the casket; it appeared to be a skeletal hand. David was ready to regurgitate his dinner. The next casket had the side missing and it was possible to see some long bones from the side. This went on until we had seen all the caskets - most of them were deteriorated with remnants (bones) of bodies showing. In another corner, we found a broken-up bookshelf and the shelves were full of small boxes - those turned out to be cremains (cremated remains) which had <u>never</u> been claimed by families.  We wondered, how old could this stuff be?  These must have been stored when the house was first built.  We were all scared, however, we still found the room to be very fascinating.  These bodies and ashes were discarded so many years ago.

We had to watch our time and this seemed like a good time to end our adventure, so we decided to return to our meeting room.  We found our way to the stairs and began to ascend them.  At about the fourth step, the plank broke and David fell through and was stuck hanging by his chest and shoulders.  As he went down, he knocked the flashlight from Charlie's hand - it fell and the light went out.  While David hung on the step, Charlie and I crawled around on the dirt floor in the dark and finally found the flashlight and turned it on again.  David wanted to scream but he knew that we couldn't afford to do that.  Charlie worked strenuously to get David loose enough so he could get a leg up.  Charlie got under David and pushed while I pulled on his shoulders to get him free.  David began to cry and we tried to calm him down.  Except for a coating of spider webs and a couple of scratches, he was unscathed.  David was able to get out and complete his climb up the stairs - more carefully this time.  Charlie and I followed closely to stay near the glow of the flashlight.  We finally reached the top and reentered the hallway and closed the door.  We spent some time catching our breath, dusting our clothes off and focused on especially, cleaning David's clothes of spider webs and dirt.  From that point, we were able to find our way out and return to the outer door and, finally, to the scout meeting.

As we looked back on our experiences in the mortuary, we realized that they were quite unique.  It provided days and days of conversation among the three of us.  As much as we wanted to share our "secrets" with our other friends, we kept it all to ourselves.  Little did we know that this experience would be reflected in our adult lives.  For one, David went on and trained to become a Mortician/Funeral Director.  The sign on the mortuary was changed to read, "Murphy and Son Mortuary."  (I always wondered if it should have read "Mrs. Murphy and Son)."  After a couple of years, David did not want to talk about it again.  I moved on to another school and it was not until several years later that I again became involved with the "death business."

\* \* \* \* \* \* \* \* \* \* \* \* \* \* \* \* \* \* \* \* \* \* \* \* \* \* \* \* \* \* \* \*

## A Bad First Day at the Office

My first employed by the mortuary was interesting; it started as a part-time position wherein I would be the first staff member to be called to remove a body from the death site.  I was excited; she was leery.

As I was working on my first day on the job, I was at the mortuary to gain more perspective on its people and functions.  I wasn't surprised when my wife  called me to ask how I was doing.  I had been there for a few hours and was given some tasks to complete.  When my wife called, I told her I was working with Mr. Hoover.  I could feel the tension in her voice as she inquired as to the cause of the death of Mr. Hoover.  I paused to hold back my laughter as I told her that I was not working on a death case, rather, I had been asked to vacuum the entire facility (with a "Hoover" vacuum cleaner).

\* \* \* \* \* \* \* \* \* \* \* \* \* \* \* \* \* \* \* \* \* \* \* \* \* \* \* \* \* \* \* \*

# 2

## The Early Years

A few years later, near the end of my time in high school, I needed to have a job. I had a paper route, which my parents decided to cancel since it was **they** who had to rise very early, first of all to get **me** up and prepare **me** to go for **my** deliveries, roll and band **my** papers to get **me** loaded in the truck and taken on **my** paper route in the snow covered roads. It would have been nearly impossible to use my bicycle since it would take me, at least, 2 and 1/2 loads - in the snow!

My next venture into the job market was at a fast food drive-in. That was great since I was able to eat anything I wanted while working. It was a very busy drive-in and I learned to do all the jobs that were necessary - even as a dishwasher. That all came to a grinding halt one day when I realized that I had forgotten to fill the ice cream machine. Well, it froze-up and the boss had to purchase a new one - that was the end of my fast-food career!

I retained my interest in the mortuary and medical business. One of my classmates had a father who was an M.D. and he helped me to get a job as an orderly at a local hospital. At first, I was assigned to a medical floor where nothing very exciting ever happened. On one day however, I was shocked when I found out that a patient I had been assisting had died. That was bad enough, but, it became worse when I was in the pathology department when a day later, I entered the morgue and found the door to the autopsy room entered and, to my shock, I saw my patient lying on the stainless steel table.

The body was lying in a pool of blood and the body cavity had been opened wide. All the organs had been removed. I moved in for a closer look and was amazed at what I saw. The bright red look of the tissue was prominent, and there was a curious odor in the air; it was a combination of chemicals and tissue and blood. I could see the ribs and the spine - everything else had been removed. As I moved up to the head, I realized that the brain had also been removed. What a moment - at that instant, I was in awe of the intricacy of the body and the fact that God had created our marvelous bodies and I wondered how it could be that I was looking at something that had until recently been a living and breathing human being. It now lay there in a frozen position - totally inert. I was totally fascinated, I returned to the morgue on the next day. I was able to talk to the assistant (another orderly, like me) and ask questions about what they did in this department. He told me about autopsies as he showed me around and led me to a display of jars with tissues in them. He said that these were the tissue samples that had been taken from the last patient (the one I had known on the medical floor). He showed me lung, liver, brain, kidney, pancreas and all the other tissues they had removed. He said that those tissues would be sent to the Histology department where they would make medical slides for the Doctor to examine microscopically in order to make a finding as to the cause of death. Wow! I was so excited I asked him if I could get a job with him in that department. He said he would tell his boss and get me on the waiting list for a job.

In the meanwhile, the hospital job was getting more and more interesting. In my travels around the hospital, I would return to the pathology area to watch the pathology procedures (autopsies) and, on my breaks, I would sneak into the surgical department to try to see some actual surgery. The more proper name for the procedure is Necropsy). There were many days when I would stay after work in order to watch a surgical procedure or an autopsy. This piqued my interest and I told my friend's Doctor father that I would like to become a doctor. He sat me down in his office and explained the process of applying, getting into a medical school. He scared me when he said that after basic medical schooling, internships and residency and specialized pathology studies, it would take 10-12 years, or more - Wow!

However, he excited me greatly since I thought that that would be a perfect plan and direction for me to take. I showed him some of the medical drawings I had made to indicate the seriousness of my interest. I had become enthralled with the work of Frank Netter - a renowned and highly acclaimed medical illustrator. The Doctor, of course, knew of Netter's work and he thought that I had shown some artistic talent which highlighted my interest in the medical field; he told me that there was another growing area of medical study I could consider - that of - Medical Illustration.

The hospital was near my house and I was able to continue working as an orderly for over a year. It was neat; I was able to wear a white outfit and "hang around" with doctors and nurses. I worked for various nurse stations and helped to move patients and attend to their needs. Medical floors were OK, but I found real excitement when I worked on the surgical floor. WOW! I was able to witness surgical procedures - even after my work hours. My parents wondered what had happened to me many times when I had stayed for an extended time. Between surgery, the morgue (autopsy room) and the emergency room, I was having the time of my life.

One day after a surgery had gone wrong, I was told to take the patient to the morgue. That is when I, again, discovered the Pathology Department. I managed to get into the autopsy room to watch my first actual necropsy (this is the scientific name for autopsy). I was amazed to see the inner parts of human beings and being awed by the work of God's hand in the creation of such a being. It made me wonder, again, in awe, how it could be that this person was recently a living and breathing human being and now he was totally inert. I noted the intricacy of the body within the open cavity. I think that that was the moment when I felt that I really wanted to become a physician and pathologist.

When I went home that night, I searched through an encyclopedia to find out all about it. While searching, I noted the beautiful illustrations of body systems and anatomical illustrations. As a budding artist, I began to try to sketch some of these illustrations on my own. I continued to be enthralled with the work of Frank Netter. I continued to add more sketches to my sketchbook. Then one day, I was in the hospital medical waste disposal area and I noticed several body parts in it. I couldn't resist it; I took a partial "human hand." I wrapped it in plastic and took it home so I could try to sketch from an actual body part. In my room, I mounted it on a cork board and dissected it carefully; pinned the skin back on the board and separated blood vessels from the muscle tissue so I could delve into it deeper. I had the best of two worlds - anatomy and illustration. It was great, at first, but after a day or so, it began to decay and emitted a bad aroma - (I used a lot of spray deodorant in the room). Of course my grandmother sensed it and came up to my room to see what was happening. When she saw what I was doing, she shrieked and immediately demanded that I dispose of my "treasure." I tried to explain the situation about the medical waste area at the hospital and she told me to stay out of that area and to <u>NEVER bring anything like that home again</u>. As a result of this, I had to leave my orderly job at the hospital and looked for something else (acceptable to my mom).

**A New Job**

One day I ran into my old friend, Charlie. I told him of my situations and I asked him he was still at the mortuary. When he said yes, I asked him if there was any work I could do with him at the mortuary. He thought for a second but then said yes, I think we have something you could do. I must have jumped ten feet high - I told him that I would be excited to do that, but, it would require special effort to be able to convince my mom that it would be a good idea. It did take quite an effort, but, since it was with my old friend, Charlie, she relented.

My first days at the mortuary were interesting, exciting and memorable. I knew that it was a situation where I, of course, didn't work, per se, in the 'prep room' where they prepared the bodies. That took special training. My duties included washing funeral vehicles, vacuuming the casket the room, the chapel and the offices, dusting and polishing caskets, accepting deliveries of flowers, unloading and moving bodies and other types of funeral support items and general upkeep of the mortuary building and support of its various functions. My favorite chore was taking the trash from the 'prep room' out to the garbage dumpster. In that action, I could see the embalmers at work - I tended to move in v-e-r-y slow motion as I performed my tasks. I was able to see various aspects of the embalming procedure. I really enjoyed what I was doing. (It reminded me of that day in Charlie's basement).

One day, Charlie asked me if I would like to be a part-time baby sitter. I told him I knew nothing about children. He laughed at me since I didn't know what he meant by that, so, I asked him why he was laughing at me. He said that he did not mean babysitting children - what he meant was very different. He said that they had to maintain a 24-hour telephone service at the mortuary and that meant that they wanted someone to stay at the mortuary office after hours (and overnight) to answer the telephone and take death calls. I immediately jumped at the chance to do it - of course, I had to get permission from my parents. Of course, they were not very enthralled at this 'opportunity' for me, but I convinced them that I would have more time to do my homework in a quiet environment and I would get home in time to get ready for school. After a lot of questions and reluctance (on my family's part), they agreed to let me do it for two nights per week. Charlie agreed to that and I became an "official mortuary baby-sitter."

For my first night on duty, Charlie stayed to help me "learn the ropes." It seemed pretty straight-forward - answer the phone, take the information down and notify the funeral director. Beyond that, I had all the time to complete my homework - and I would get extra pay. Oh, and he said, **<u>Do Not Say Thank You after taking</u>**

**a death call!**  (I hadn't thought of that).

After a coupe of training sessions, the time came when I was to be there on my own.  It was great - I was feeling very important.  After supper, I headed to the mortuary on my bike.  I met Charlie there; he greeted me and got me settled into the office chair and placed the rolodex on the desk in the event I needed a number.  He departed and there I was - Mr. Important!  The hours ticked away and there were no calls.  I studied my homework and, eventually, began to get tired of homework, so, I began to wander around inside the mortuary.  I had to stay within reach of the phone. It was fairly dark, except for some night-lights in the slumber rooms, so I took a flashlight with me.  I knew that Charlie and his family were there, sleeping on the third floor, but it was still quite spooky.  I thought that this could be my chance to see the upstairs 'prep room, (I already knew about the one in the basement) all to myself, so, I headed in that direction.  On the way, I found two reposing rooms which had the bodies lying in coffins - of course, I had to take a look.  It was an eerie sight; these were bodies prepared for funeral services the next day.  Now I realized why they called this job "baby sitting."

I reached the door of the "prep room" and entered quietly - WHY QUIETLY? (My "babies" were not going to hear anything!)  As I entered, I noted all the cabinetry with drawers full of surgical-looking instruments.  There were two embalming tables; one of them was occupied and covered with a white sheet.  I lifted the end of the sheet to see the body.  It looked normal; it was a pale pink - it had already been embalmed and dressed nicely.  It was ready for casketing in the morning.  I returned to the office to resume my sentry-like duties.  I didn't realize how quiet and dark this place could become.  After I completed my homework, I searched for something to do in the office.  I scanned catalogues and even the telephone book.

Suddenly, the telephone rang!!!  I jumped and nearly fell off the chair - after all this quiet, the sudden shrill of the telephone was very alarming.  I tried to compose myself, then answered the phone and, with a somewhat shaky voice, took my first death call and followed through all the procedures.  Wow, what a moment.  After I calmed down, I felt pretty proud of my performance.  After a few weeks of this duty, I managed to work without fear and anticipation. (I always wondered if I had said "Thank You" for that first death call).  I managed to compose myself and telephoned the on-call 'remover' to report the death and the need for a removal and tell him whether to bring it to the mortuary or take it to the Medical Examiner.  If he were to bring it to the mortuary, I would be there to help him unload and place the body on a gurney and roll it into the prep room for the morning shift to begin work on it.

Later, I was allowed to enter the "prep room" and I was finally allowed to observe the actual embalming process. I was full of questions; I asked how I could be trained to do that. They told me that it required attendance at a 2-year embalming school to train to do this. It was very memorable and it reminded me of that night in the basement when I witnessed my first body preparation. It was really very interesting because of my friend, Charlie; without him this may have never been possible. I remembered all the times we had as we had once played hide and seek in that building and we remembered all the good times we had together.

One day, at the mortuary, we were expecting the laundry man to pick up the used sheets. It was a great opportunity to pull a prank. We moved the full laundry bins and placed them between the embalming tables (they were usually placed at the entry to the 'prep room') then waited until the laundry truck drove up - Charlie removed his shoes and socks, hoisted his pant legs, hopped up onto one of the embalming tables and covered himself with a sheet - with only his feet showing. I greeted the laundry man and led him into the prep room - I could see his fearful anticipation and he slowly entered the room. This time, he had to collect the laundry bin from between the embalming tables. When he saw the covered body on the table, he withdrew noticeably and tiptoed toward the laundry bin at a very deliberate and slow pace. After he had passed the halfway point, Charlie moved and raised his arm pulling the sheet from his face. The laundry man froze, turned pale and made a rapid u-turn and fled the room with a scream. He nearly knocked me down as he darted out of the door and ran down the block - he left his truck - I don't know if he ever returned to that job or how the truck was retrieved. Needless to say, Charlie and I roared with laughter after that incident.

I really enjoyed my job at the mortuary. As a result, I began to seriously consider the possibility of attending an embalming school and the mortuary owner also encouraged me to consider it seriously.

On another day, I assisted with a funeral; I helped load a body into a casket, watched while the make-up was 'touched-up,' arranged the chapel with flowers, moved the casket into the chapel on a bier, checked the sound system and loaded the music, then drove the flower car to the cemetery set up the gravesite.

It had been raining all night and it was still falling, though lightly; the ground was very mushy. I had to park on the road and that caused me to have a fairly long walk to the gravesite several times to unload and carry all of the flowers. The entire way was soft as my feet sunk into the soggy ground. After I set all the flowers in place under the graveside canopy, I waited until the funeral procession arrived. It was still raining slightly. I stood back and out of site as the hearse backed up to the grave. As the Funeral Director approached the back door of the hearse and opened it and unlocked the casket holders, the car began to sink into the soft ground. Before long the bumper touched the ground and the casket began to slide out. The assistants and some of the men in attendance grabbed for it, but, it was too late. It had gained momentum and soon it slid out completely and into the grave. It lay there at an angle and no one could move it; they were sinking and sliding all over the place and they certainly did not want to get into the grave to move it.

The cemetery office was called and they said they would send out a ground crew. The Funeral Director decided to go on with the graveside service as the rain increased and everyone huddled under the small canopy. After the service was completed, three of us remained behind to help realign the casket and get it set in place properly (some of the funeral attendees also stayed to help). It was nearly impossible because of the rain - we were completely soaked! The back-hoe which the office sent, was usually used for such procedures as lifting caskets but it was unable to be used due to the ground conditions. Several of the men helped as we tried to move the hearse forward manually, but, the spinning wheels splashed mud over almost everyone. With straps, hooks and several men, we were able to finally get the casket to settle.

I was asked to go down into the grave to open the casket and make certain that the body was in its proper place. First, I had to locate the "key" (crank) to unseal the top of the casket which had been tightened at the end of the funeral service. I used the crank to unseal the top and tried to get to the lid open, however, it was frozen and I could not move the lid. With the help of the men who had helped move the hearse, we managed to shove and push and pull until we could get the casket to lay flat on the vault slab at the bottom of the grave which, by now was not visible due to the pooling of rainwater. I located the lid latch and, with a great deal, of effort, managed to get the lid open and to stay up while I tried to reconfigure the corpse; this would have been nearly impossible at first. I was so wet and muddy; I could not help but mar the interior of the casket and the clothing of the deceased as I attempted to realign his position. I had heard of stories where a hearse had backed into the grave, but this event reminded me not to laugh at such stories.

## A New Location

Upon graduation from high school, I received a baseball scholarship which caused me to move out of town. That trumped my idea of entering embalming school. I continued to work at the mortuary through the summer months. One day, the owner asked me to run an errand to the town where I planned to attend college - how fortunate. He wanted me to take a couple of packages to the mortuary there. I gladly agreed to do it since I was going to spend my next four years there and it would give me a chance to, not only, look at the school but also to meet the people who worked at the mortuary and find out about the possibility of a part-time job at the mortuary there. I thought I could get a part-time job there while attending college.

I drove to that town (in one of the large funeral cars), located the college area and then proceeded to the nearby mortuary where I was to deliver the packages. I walked up to the door and rang the bell. There was a young college-aged-looking man who answered the door and greeted me nicely. I told him that I represented the mortuary in my town; I gave him the packages and he was very gracious. I told him that I was working at the mortuary at my home town and was going to attend the college in his town. I also told him that I was interested in medical school but that I also had considered embalming college. I asked him for a tour of his facility. He said that his time was limited, since he was working on some cases, but, he would be willing to let me watch him in the 'prep room.' I thought that that was great!

He led me through the chapel and down the hallway to the 'prep room.' As I entered the very large room, he presented me with a mask, an apron and some rubber gloves. I saw four embalming tables, which were manned by several people working on bodies. "What a huge operation! It was fascinating to me as I was told that the bodies were there as the result of a bus-train accident and many of the bodies had been dismembered. The embalmers were trying to match parts in order to get bodies properly complete. After they had determined which parts were matched appropriately, they proceeded to embalm each part separately. After all the parts were embalmed and collected together, they were placed into plastic bags

27

and packed with an embalming powder and sealed. The bodies in the plastic bags would later be placed into caskets or cremated. Because of their condition, viewing of these remains would not be possible by the families. Others were prepared in the normal manner and designated as 'viewable.'

This process further piqued my interest in this work. I thanked my guide profusely as I prepared to return home. I thanked him for the wonderful opportunity to observe the process of dealing with dismembered bodies. He stopped me briefly and asked me to take a return package to my boss. He also said that I was welcome to contact him when I returned to attend college and that he might find an opportunity for me to work in his mortuary part-time. I was very excited about that possibility.

When summer ended, I left home and headed off to college. I was very excited and additionally looked forward to working in the mortuary in the new city. Since I had the baseball scholarship, I was given a mandatory part-time job in the athletics department. That limited any time I would have had available to work at the mortuary. I did make a couple of visits, but, I (unfortunately), I did not have the time to work there. During the baseball season, there was baseball practice every day and games at home and away. Another detraction arose when I developed my interest in the ROTC Program. That was another interest which involved many days of participation (especially after my classes had concluded - and on weekends). As a result, my advancement in the mortuary business was interrupted. The closest I came to mollifying my interest in the scientific aspect of what I had done before, was when I became an Art major and specialized in illustration, watercolor and sculpture. That gave me the opportunity to delve into more medical illustration. It also piqued my interest in sculpture as related to facial and hand reconstruction in the mortuary business. While there, in my third year, I was able to complete some illustrations for an Anatomy and Physiology professor who was writing a book. He used some of my drawings in his Anatomy book. After that, because of all my Commission in the USAF, I left immediately after graduation and from that time, I was moving around frequently, so, I was unable to continue with that project.

The four years of college had passed rapidly and because I had entered the ROTC program, I was commissioned as an officer and set for immediate entry into the United States Air Force. Again, my mortuary career was sidelined. However, it did not stop me completely - while assigned to my very first Air Force Base, I contacted the Base Mortuary Officer and shirt-tailed him to learn his job as he visited mortuaries where deceased airmen were taken and prepared for funerals or shipment. In addition, I was able to accompany him to homes where he had to inform relatives of the loss of their husbands, fathers etc. to inform them of the procedures the Air Force would undertake (sic) to monitor the shipment and/or local rites for their loved one.

At another base, I found a part-time job in a local mortuary. My early training in Charlie's mortuary was a great help. My experience there was pretty routine, but because I had not attended an embalming school, I was not able to perform any embalmings unassisted, however, I assisted in many cases very closely. I was also able to get a position as Assistant Base Mortuary Officer and participated in many cased where I was sent to aircraft crash sites to oversee removal of air crewmen and transported them to the base where we then had to determined the disposition of the remains. (Fortunately, I had learned much of the job at my earlier base). We contacted the families and assisted in the procedural arrangements. In some cases, we had to transport the remains to a medical examiner where a necropsy could be performed. In that job, with the Air Force, I was able to have experience with air crash military victims that had either been in our area or shipped in from other areas. Most of the cases involved death by burning and some had died from the impact with the ground where no flames had occurred. At this point, I had only an affiliated relationship with the mortuaries. The bodies were sent (or taken) to the various mortuaries and it allowed me to witness the different methods of body preparation and disposal of them as a result of aircraft crashes.

The burn cases were more difficult so, in general, the cases required closed-casket preparation; that is where the body could not be viewed. Those bodies were examined by a forensic pathologist who searched for trauma from injuries which had been caused by the crash; he also took fluid specimens to test for drugs and/or alcohol. After the body was released to the mortuary, it became their job to take care of the final disposition. In the case of a severely burned body, the mortician used the trocar tube to probe and release gases then he attempted to locate any vessels which can accept a cannula where the embalming fluid could be pumped into it. It usually entailed several entry points, however, they were usually dead-end (so to speak) entries.

After the mortician embalmed as much as he could, (much of it with the trocar) the body was powdered heavily, placed in a double plastic heavy-duty sheet and then wrapped in plastic.  Before closing the plastic completely, embalming powder is heavily sprinkled in and around the complete body and the plastic was closed and made as air-tight as possible.  The body was then placed in a casket which would have been chosen by the family or in a Ziegler case, which was a metal casket-looking container suitable for shipping - it was sealed in front of an Air Force Officer - usually the Air Base Mortuary Officer, loaded into a hearse for transport to the airport or to the cemetery.  (We also arrange for an airman to escort the body to its destination).  In cases were the trauma was not so severe, the body was sent to the Forensic Lab where further forensic tests would be performed.

One of the major functions of the Mortuary Officer was to make initial contact with the family of the deceased military member to offer condolences and to discuss any specific requests the family might have regarding, disposal, church and cemetery services and veterans benefits and other concerns.  These are usually very standard visits and business can be completed efficiently - we did not want to expedite everything at the expense of a family in mourning.

This reminded me of a case where I accompanied a Medical Examiner's case-worker to notify a family of the loss of their teenage daughter who had been killed in a traffic accident.  It was a very emotional moment.  After my partner had expressed great sympathy about the daughter, the father said, "What do you mean, my daughter?"  "I received word that my **son** had been killed in a traffic accident only hours ago."  After a quick call to the lab, my partner confirmed that the parents had lost both teenage children on the same evening.  I never wanted to go on those trips again.

\* \* \* \* \* \* \* \* \* \* \* \* \* \* \* \* \* \* \* \* \* \* \* \* \* \* \* \* \* \* \* \* \*

### Which way out?
It was a service for a deceased man from the middle east.  It was a rush job since the family believed in burial within 24 hours of the death.  That was bad enough, but, when the elders began to argue about the location of Mecca.  Each time they thought they knew the direction, the casket on the bier was turned so that the head would face that way.  As they continued to dispute the way to turn the casket to what they had thought was Mecca, the casket continued to spin like a top.

\* \* \* \* \* \* \* \* \* \* \* \* \* \* \* \* \* \* \* \* \* \* \* \* \* \* \* \* \* \* \* \*

# 3

## What is Forensics?

At the end of my Active Duty in the Air Force, I decided to transfer to the Reserve Air Force. In anticipation of a new job, I moved my family to another State. When I arrived, I ran into a hiring freeze for my chosen vocation. As I searched for another interim position, I found a mortuary that offered me an apartment and a job as an apprentice embalmer. Unfortunately, my family was uncomfortable with the thought of living over a mortuary, so I had to turn the offer down. My next stop was at the State University. I found a position as a 'diener' (Also known as an Autopsy Technician) (Diener is German for Servant or Greek for Slave). I would work in the University Pathology Department and assist in autopsies (Necropsies) as a dissector which assists the pathologist, in this case, a legal pathologist known as a Medical Examiner) with the removal of organs so as to study the various vital parts to determine the cause of death. The Medical Examiner is the pathologist who examines cases of unknown death or legal cases which involved homicide. (I will be using the term autopsy to refer to the process),

Most of the cases were for persons who had died as an unattended death, whereby no physician had monitored the person at the time of death; there have been many situations where deaths have occurred as a result of unknown causes. This is the world of Forensic Pathology - where causes of death are determined for family members, for insurance payment determination and for the legal system by a forensic pathologist (Medical Examiner). In some places, a Coroner is an appointee/electee of the State Government whose function is to hold hearings to investigate and seek to determine the causes of unknown death cases. He or she may not necessarily be a physician. The Medical Examiner, on the other hand, is a trained medical Doctor of Pathology who specialize (through additional training) in Forensic Medicine. As mentioned before, these cases ca be very interesting since it is quite possible that the originally perceived cause of death may turn out to be as a result of another cause. For example, a decedent who came in with large holes in the skull was perceived to have been shot a close range - after the postmortem forensic examination, it was determined that the holes were as a result of tertiary cancer which had eaten away at the cranium.

As a side job in the Pathology department, I also managed the hospital pathology museum where significant body parts were preserved for medical students to study. It included photography and bagged/plasticized parts for archives. I received on-the-job training and became fully qualified as a medical museum curator as well as an autopsy technician. In this function, I mounted specific organs or organ parts and photographed them on a stand where a camera was mounted. My photos were frequently used for pathology conferences where pathologists would discuss the cases in detail. There was also a weekly "Brain Conference" where my mounted specimens would again be discussed in great detail.

The Medical Examiner, through the Pathology Office also employed a Special Investigator whose task was to visit the crime/accident scene to make notes on everything surrounding the death. He described the crime scene and tried to give the doctor a sense of 'being there.' He also took photographs at the scene. His notes and photos provided insight for the Pathologist as he progressed through the entire autopsy. When the autopsy was concluded, he (the Doctor) corroborated all the notes and other information with the autopsy findings to isolate the actual cause of death through a mental reconstruction of the death scene - he was also provided photographs of the scene from the police photographer. At the end, he would make a determination as to the cause of death and sign the death certificate. The body was then sent to a funeral home.

I worked on many interesting case and learned a great deal about anatomy, disease and accident investigation. I will never forget the sense of awe I had when I was the one who opened the bodies on the autopsy table. It was just as before, yet, somehow different. I continued to be amazed at the intricacy of the body and how it all works together - the only thing missing was the 'soul.'

In one instance, I was asked if I wanted to accompany the forensic investigator to a death scene. I jumped at the opportunity. I imagined all sorts of scenarios, murder, suicide, drowning and every other sort of death. If it were drowning, I could test the theory that females float frontside up and males float rear-end up.

I donned a forensic pathology suit (similar to a flight suit used in military aviation), jumped into the van. The police had already preceded us and were there taking photos and making measurements at the site. It was a case where a woman had died in her car in her garage with the motor running. I was asked to help remove her from the driver's seat. I donned a mask and double-gloves and quickly moved to the driver's side, opened the door and noticed a strong odor emanating from inside the car (the windows had been closed). She was a large woman and because she had bloated; her skin was blotchy and discolored - a strong sign of putrefaction (decomposition); (apparently since she had been dead for several hours or, perhaps a day or two) she was tightly pressed between the seat and the steering wheel. There was also the strong smell of automobile fumes. I thought that I could just pull her out, but to my surprise, she had already begun to decompose and my hands went right through the arm tissues to the bone and when I pulled I began to strip the skin and muscle tissue from her arm as if I were stripping the meat from the bone. My gloved hands and my sleeves were covered with her fluids and tissues. It was decided to move the chair back further in order to release her from her trapped position (Why didn't I think of that???).

This was just one of the many experiences I had with extricating dead victims from crime or accident scenes. On that same day, when I returned to the lab, we were notified that an ambulance was bringing in a homeless victim found in an alley. When he arrived, we had some difficulty placing him on the autopsy table since he had died while in a fetal position (apparently sleeping). He had reached full Rigor Mortis and we couldn't begin the autopsy until we could lay him out straight. This meant that we had to go around his body and snap every joint (breaking all the tendons which had stiffened - his fingers, arms legs, torso head and neck) until we could get him into a flat position.

In my role as a pathology assistant, I also coordinated with the Police Department regarding deaths within their area of authority. The experiences I had with the Forensic Pathology Department were invaluable - murders (shootings, stabbings, fires, electrocutions, premature birth, etc.) Even though we had such disparate cases, I learned that there is really only one cause of death; heart stoppage.

In the Forensic Autopsy, there are other aspects which more specifically identify the cause of death. These are classified: (S.H.A.N.U) i.e., Suicide, Homicide, Accident, Natural and, finally, Unknown - these are called the 'manner' of death. It was very interesting to realize that the appearance of a cause of death may not be the actual cause. I was involved in a case where the body had a major crushing of the head, which seemed like the obvious cause of death. After the autopsy, it was found that the man had had a heart attack while working on a roof, fell to the ground and fractured his skull. In another case, we had to determine the cause of death of a person who was retrieved from a car in the river. He was under water

33

for an extended period of time and the cause of death again seemed obvious (drowning).  Again, I was surprised at the end of the examination; they had determined that the man had had a heart attack and a seizure before his automobile entered the river.  When the lungs were checked, we found that no water had been aspirated (breathed) into the lungs - therefore, no drowning.  The answer was in the heart.  Cases like this make one realize that seeing may not be believable - there is probably something underlying what your eyes won't tell you.

You may have noticed that lately, there have been a large number of television shows which show the involvement of detectives and forensic scientists.  Families have been appreciative of the work of the forensic pathologist where a cause of death has been established - many of the rulings had major implications on insurance policy payouts.  Likewise, there are many criminals who are not glad that such a profession exists.  Discovery of the DNA molecule has changed the methods of criminal investigation.

**The Autopsy**

Now, regarding the autopsy and the need for one: first of all, such procedures are covered by State Law; each State has guidelines or laws which approve/require or disapprove the procedure. If approved, the legal next of kin must sign an autopsy approval permit.  Most religions allow autopsy (Muslims prefer not to have one), orthodox Jews request to have a Rabbi present and Mormons want to have a church representative present and they have a dressing ceremony at the mortuary which involves several church officials.  If the autopsy is conducted at the funeral home, that expedites the process.  In the case of forensic autopsy, the State has to authority to approve the Medical Examiner's examination.

In general, families will approve the procedure.  In cases where they have refused, a large percentage of them have later regretted that they had not approved it.  They had to live with the missing information, which could have been discovered through an autopsy, which may never again be attainable (if the body was cremated) or, they might opt for an exhumation.  Autopsies can be accomplished after burial and, for the most part can, believe it or not, reveal nearly, the same results as it might have initially after the death.  Autopsies have been done years after burial in some cases such as for criminal cases.  It is surprising how many tissues and DNA samples can be found useful even years after burial.  Many criminal cases have been solved through examination of DNA from a previously buried body.

The term autopsy (which literally means, self-examination) can also be referred to as the Post-Mortem examination, Disambiguation, autopsia cadavera, and obduction. The autopsy procedure is utilized for various reasons:

- to determine as precisely the cause of death.
- to confirm or exclude a disease diagnosis before the death.
- to annotate disease progression.
- to document undocumented disease(s).
- to collect samples of body fluids and tissues to help the Health Department identify and the tracking of diseases for the protection of public health.
- to determine the existence of criminal activity regarding the death.

The autopsy leaves no disfigurement of the individual. With an open casket funeral, it is quite possible that the body can be viewed by the public. The mortician can use make-up to cover any surgical repairs or injuries and a pillow can be arranged around the head to conceal any autopsy marks on the head. Most autopsies are done in hospitals or Medical Examiner's Offices/Labs - (they can also be done at mortuaries and at various other types of facilities). There is no typical charge for the service. There, are, however, at the request of an immediate family member, private pathologists who will perform the procedure for a fairly significant fee and, possibility rental costs for a room or facility (some are even done in a trailer or a temporary facility which has specifically outfitted for that purpose. A small hospital may not have the appropriate facility for performing these autopsies, so, they might request a nominal fee to accomplish a procedure they do not normally house. It is not completely unusual to have an autopsy in the mortuary - in many cases, that will be the site for the performance of enucleations (eyeball removal). A fee will usually be charged for the pathologist and a technician. Morticians have the skills to restore the eyeball shape, scars, addition or removal of mustaches and many other types of changes the next of kin may want to have added or deleted with the use of makeup and Morticians Wax.

There are four types of autopsies:

- <u>Clinical</u> - done for medical reasons. It is especially done for the protection of public health.

- <u>Forensic</u> - done for legal reasons to determine the cause of an unnatural or unattended death which may involve a crime.

- <u>Anatomical</u> - academic autopsies for medical education.

- <u>Virtual Medical Imaging</u> - utilizes imaging technology - MRI and Computerization * Tomography is used.
*(Greek; Tomos = Section; Graphy = Representation)

In former days, autopsies and embalmings were done on a large table in the home. The body was laid out and, because there was no efficient means of draining the blood, they situated the arms of the corpse in an outstretched position and located buckets under each hand. Hence, the old saying: "Don't kick the bucket!"

**The Clinical Autopsy**

The Clinical type of autopsy is a surgical procedure which, typically enables physicians to study a disease as it progressed and which may have finally taken the life of a patient.

First, lets get a general overview of the procedure. There are many similarities between the two types of autopsies. The Forensic Autopsy tends to be more detailed and more inclusive because of the legal ramifications. That is because in the clinical autopsy, the general cause of death is already known and the autopsy can focus on a particular area. For the Forensic Autopsy, a possible cause is known, but more care must be taken, i.e. more surrounding issues must be considered so as to be able to defend the procedures and the results in court.

The general procedure for the Clinical Autopsy will involve a pathologist (An M.D. trained in the study of disease) and an assistant (not necessarily an M.D.), (sometimes two), smocked-up with a surgical suit, mask and gloves, cloth or plastic shoe covers. (Some dieners keep an old pair of shoes in the lab which they use exclusively during autopsies). It is also possible for such autopsies to be done by the family doctor who cared for the deceased. These can be more superficial and focus primarily on the sight of the disease in question.

It begins with an external examination of the body. The pathologist will use a scalpel (for small samples or scrapings) and measuring sticks (in centimeters) to make annotations of the size of marks or injuries or evidence of disease. He will simulate the markings and draw them on the outlined figure on his clipboard.

He begins the surgical incision with the usual "Y" incision that begins from the shoulders (ends of the clavicles) to the mid-chest (lower sternum) then (beside the navel) down to the pubic bone. After that, the assistants take over to release the skin and fat and muscle to reveal the ribs. While they do that, the pathologist moves to the head, makes a couple of cuts to open the scalp enough to reveal the saws cutting area (where the hair can be parted cleanly) and opens the skull with a vibrator saw. (The vibrator saw reduces the amount of blood, which may spatter during the cutting procedure and reduce the possibility of cutting too deeply). Of course, since there is no blood pressure, there is no circulation, so, typically, the only bleeding arises from pooled blood in certain areas.

He then carefully saws where the hair which he parts across the rear third of the skull; it creates a line across the cranium on a line above the ear. While sawing, he creates a 'notch' in each side of the skullcap and a projecting point from the lower edge of the skull so that the skullcap can be replaced perfectly after completion of the examination. This greatly helps the mortician to align the skull halves to present a natural look. If, for some medical reason, the skullcap is retained by the pathologist or the pathologist does not create an alignment notch, the mortician's job becomes more difficult. If the skullcap is missing, he has to replace the shape of the top of the head with cotton or other materials to rebuild the shape of the top of the head. If the skull cap has no alignment notches, he will have to estimate the position of the skull cap and glue it in place. In ether case, he will then pull the scalp back into place and sew at the hairline to complete the closure.

After the pathologist exposes the brain, he carefully examines it externally. He may take small samples while it is still in place. He will also remove the pituitary gland and have it saved for the research lab. In other situations, he might continue and remove the entire brain and either slice it and weigh it and place the complete brain in a container of fluid for later examination. Typically, in a case involving a "medical" death, the brain, typically will not be removed unless it is the focus of the examination.

While he is examining the head and removing brain, the dieners begin to remove the organs of the torso. It is also possible for a diener to remove the brain, as directed by the pathologist. The doctor will return to examine the open chest and abdomen and cranuim. We begin by removing the breastplate using a large long-handled cutting tool (similar to a hedge-cutter). The cuts are made where the ribs and the sternum are connected with cartilage. The breastplate is released by using a scalpel to separate it from the underlying tissues. At that point, one can view the lungs, heart, liver and other organs in situ. The process continues and each organ is removed, weighed and set aside in an organized fashion where the doctor can examine each one closely.

After the dieners have completed the removal work, the doctor returns to the torso area, which has been cleared for examination. He looks over the area to locate any trauma or disease. He can inspect the underside of bruising, broken ribs and other types of trauma to the torso. He will weigh each organ to identify abnormalities. As he inspects each organ and cuts slices from them and places them into small jars of liquid for later toxicological testing. He even directs the dieners to save the stomach contents and remove and open the stomach and he wants to see the bowel contents bowels and he inspects the inner surfaces of the stomach and intestines.

As he searches the body tissues, he selects tissue samples; if he notices lesions or large lumps, he may remove large segments and save them for later microscopic examination. In general, he will collect samples of bile, eye fluid and small samples of brain, liver, and other organs. The organ tissue samples and body fluids may reveal the presence of alcohol, poisons or street drugs.

By contrast, in the clinical autopsy, the pathologist is specifically searching for areas around the reported cause of death as reported from an attending physician. If that includes the heart, he will remove it and dissect it. All organs are weighed. He will section the coronary arteries and areas of disease and save samples. He will do this with all suspected organs and he places the remains into a plastic bag which will be stored in the body cavity. At the conclusion of all sample removal, the body is sewn up (with the unused tissues inside of a plastic bag; the body is than taken to cold storage until the mortician is summoned to remove it).

When internal organs are removed, there is a separation of the arteries and veins at the arms and legs. Because the embalming which will occur later, it will be important for the embalmer to retrieve the ends of those vessels at each point - when cut, they tend to withdraw into the limbs. It is most helpful if the dieners would tie off those vessels so that the embalmer can locate them rapidly. When they are cut properly, the diener will use about 10 inches of ligature (string) to tie-off the vessels and the string ends will protrude (even though the vessels have withdrawn) and they can be used to pull the vessels out so that the embalming procedure can proceed. The ends of the vessels can be found and a cannula can be inserted easily. As a diener, I always made certain that vessels were tied-off and long strings were available to the embalmer.

**The Forensic Autopsy**

This was introduced in the first part of this chapter. Forensic Pathology has become very prominent in the news today. It is frequently emulated in various television shows. My first exposure to that was Dr. Quincy, M.D. As mentioned earlier, Forensic Autopsy is performed when there is a case of a death from an unknown cause or as related to a criminal violent death. It differs from a normal (clinical) autopsy inasmuch as it is searching for evidence of criminal or accidental death. I received on-the-job training as a diener. Of course, it was important to know and understand anatomy so to avoid total embarrassment. I was trained to especially recognize that the autopsy procedure is a very serious scientific procedural examination and that all seriousness for respect and dignity of the individual are paramount. This procedure can become very involved and intricate; this, however, this description will highlight the general procedures - remember, we are looking for evidence of violent or other non-natural death. The real charge is to locate the truth as related to the death. In a legal situation, the pathologist may be called to testify in court, therefore, he is very meticulous in his approach to the post-mortem examination. There was a case where an attorney asked the M.E. if he had done a complete autopsy. The M.E. responded in the affirmative. The lawyer proceeded to ask him about the condition of the sinus cavities. As you can see, the thoroughness in a criminal case is vital. When the M.E. said that he had not examined them, the case was thrown out.

It is a great career if you like to find answers to problematic situations. In the field of forensic pathology, the underlying cause of death may not be what the obvious indicators may suggest. Many autopsy rooms have a sign hanging on the wall or door which reads: *"Hoc locus est ubi mors gaudet seccurrere vitae"* which means, "This is the place where death rejoices to help those who live."

In the beginning, we establish a team of at least two or three dieners who will work in tandem since many sets of eyes can help to ascertain that all possible different abnormalities are noted - it also expedites the procedure. We need to protect ourselves with our smocks and masks or facial shields and shoe covers.  I liked to double-glove to assure protection from contact with diseased tissues and fluids.  Of course, these won't protect you from a cut from a sharp bone fragment through the gloves or from yourself when cutting in non-visible areas (where you can't see your hands).  Masks are either cloth or more extensive with a breathing mask.  These are invaluable when working with a body which has a severe odor from decomposition or other necrosis.

The medical instruments are all lined up on a stainless steel cart or counter so that the doctor can have easy access to them.  The pathologist will do the detailed dissection of each organ personally and retain whatever samples he wishes to explore further.  The dieners assist him an any way possible.

The doctor (pathologist) begins with an external examination.  The doctor's review of the notes from the onsite investigator regarding the crime scene or accident location will have provided him with a great amount of information.  He also wants to confirm the identity of the individual - a diener will take a photograph, another will take fingerprints.  The doctor annotates hair color and length, eye color, scars, tattoos or other identification marks; he may collect a hair sample and scrapings from under the nails.  He will also look for paint flakes or gunpowder stains to collect other samples.  He examines the hands and arms for evidence of defense wounds.  He also examines the clothes carefully for dirt, tears, and body fluid stains, etc.  He also compares the report of the onsite investigator and examines the on-scene photographs to determine the body position at death.  He might even visit the crime scene to gather further information.  When possible, he also obtains any medical records which might be available.  He assures that the families are contacted.

During this exterior examination, he examines the body for any marks or clues toward determining the cause of death (and identification).  I would be there to turn the body so the doctor can see the backside of the body.  I would stand on the opposite side of the table, reach over the body, grasp the other side of it and pull it toward me until the body was lying on its side.  The doctor made written notes on a pad with body outlines on it so he could replicate the areas where he found injury or identification marks; he also spoke into a microphone to record his observations.  He wants to determine whether the examination is related to a criminal causes or whether the death was a suicide.

He obtained the weight of the body from the intake office, which weighed the body on the gurney when first delivered. I measured the length of the body for him. I retrieved a lab camera and took a photograph of the head and, perhaps wounds. Of course, I would have to call him in the event I came across something unusual. Regarding the removal of the organs, there are several different techniques to the job of extricating the organs. The first one was called the **Rokitanski Method** wherein the organs are removed as a 'total' unit where tall the organs remained in situ (it its original place) and the doctor would then remove the sections he wanted to examine more closely. For some cases, the doctor did need to see certain parts that had been a part of the injury or illness - so, he could then be selective in his organ examination - this would be the **Virchow Method**. This was a bit risky however, since the M.E. was frequently called to testify in many cases. There was the possibility that a lawyer would <u>not</u> consider it a <u>complete</u> autopsy unless each and every organ had been examined thoroughly (even with a GSW) (gun shot wound) to the head?). The other method involves a diligent removal of <u>each </u>organ, empty of contents and cleaned for the doctor to examine. There is also the **Letulle Method,** which offered a step-by-step way to proceed through the body organs.

As in the Clinical Autopsy, the first incision is shaped like a 'Y' which begins at the outer end of each clavicle (right and left), meets a the bottom of the sternum and proceeds at a downward angle to the center of the body (around the navel) to the lower part of the sternum. This presents as a 'V' at the upper part of the incision. At the lower point of the V, the incision proceeds downward the midline toward the pelvis (avoiding the navel) to the pubic bone. The chest and abdominal flaps can then be pulled back to reveal the ribs and the abdominal organs.

The procedure continues as in the Clinical Autopsy but with more detailed look or detailed examination of parts where trauma, signs of disease or unusual damage may be located. Remember, this is a case regarding an unnatural or undetermined death. In most forensic cases, the procedure continues until all the organs have been removed and separated. The pathologist examines and weighs each organ and dissects each of them looking for trauma or disease. He will also slice a portion each organ off and place them in small jars of fluid. These samples will be sent to Histology for slide preparation (for microscopic examination) and to Toxicology to determine the presence of alcohol or drugs. When that part of the autopsy is concluded all the remaining tissues (including any unsaved brain tissue) are placed in a plastic bag and <u>loosely</u> sewn into the body cavity. (The mortician will have to access that area next).

If it wasn't done first, the brain is removed. I first make a cut across the head from the back of the top of the ears and make a cut over the back third of the head (while parting the hair neatly). The scalp is not totally removed but the cut allows the scalp to be drawn back into place when the skullcap is replaced. I pull the two parts of the scalp back to reveal the top of the skull.

Morticians prefer to have the notch(es) on the side to avoid any problems with the forehead during the final preparation and make-up stage. The vibrator saw vibrates the blade and that keep you from cutting into the brain underneath the bone. When the cut is completed, the skullcap is removed carefully realizing that the dura mater is attached to it and must be carefully separated from it. The diener reaches inside under the brain with both hands to the brainstem and from that point snips the brainstem and the connecting vessels and other tissue until the brain can be removed carefully. The skullcap is then removed and set aside for later replacement. The dura mater also is saved in a solution.

One must be very careful when making the blind cut at the brain stem. This is a blind cut since your hands are hidden inside the brain cavity - one hand holds the brain and the other hand is using a scalpel. It is possible to cut yourself when you reach down an under the brain. The brain surface is very soft and it is easy to place a finger into it - that doesn't destroy the brain nor does it hamper the pathologist in his analysis, but you want to remove it without injury if possible. It might be a case where the brain will later be sliced and prepared for slides or for another type of presentation, so, holes would not be a good thing. Once removed, the brain is placed on a cork board where the pathologist can examine it carefully. He might slice it into cross-section slabs and remove the pituitary gland). I can now replace the skull cap and it will be in place because of the location notch(es) I created when I first cut it. The scalp can now be stretched and returned to its normal position, the hair combed back and loosely sewn shut. It is loose so that the mortician can treat the inside of the cranium and stuff it with cotton to avoid leakage. The loose sewing allows him to get into it easier - he will then seal it and sew it tighter in position when the body is prepared for final viewing. The sewn cut is somewhat to the rear of the head so the natural hair can cover it and a small pillow can be placed in a position so as to hide evidence of the autopsy.

The autopsy procedure creates a problem for the mortician. Instead of one incision to embalm from the jugular vein, it will now require several entry points for the cannula. The full autopsy has destroyed the natural circulatory system. At this point, you have an open cavity where you have five (possibly ten) embalming entry points, one artery/vein for each arm and one artery/vein for each leg and one artery/vein for each side of the head. Each entry requires me to locate the arteries and veins for each point for insertion of the cannula. This constitutes a very time-consuming procedure compared to the normal one or two-entry case.

Again, when one looks at an open body like this and the cavity is empty with the various organs nearby in a plastic bag, one can only marvel at the wonder of Gods' work. To consider that only hours ago, this was a living and breathing human being and now with the organs in the body cavity missing, (as I remembered my first vision of this when I was an orderly); it is an amazing contemplation. This illustrates one reason that people enter this field; it is to show the appreciation of life and to offer an important service - to take care of the remains of their loved one at the time of his/her death in a dignified and honorable way. Their purpose is to handle the remains and the survivors in such a way as to give great homage to the deceased and to render all necessary services to the families. I approached it with the attitude that this could be my own family member.

After the pathologist has completed the dissection process and collection of data. The body is then transferred to the mortuary for embalming and final preparation the funeral service. At the end of the embalming procedure on a body that has had an autopsy, the conclusion of the procedure will involve completion of the facial formation and mouth closure, the loose organ tissues are retrieved from the body cavity and embalmed with a trocar tube, (a long hollow steel tube with a sharp point and one end and a connecting thread on the other), then, the tissues are placed in a plastic bag and powdered thoroughly with an embalming powder (hexaphene anti-fungal germicidal) and repacked into the body cavity. The bag is returned to the body cavity and it is sewn together (leak-proofed/sealed) to present a normal shape. It is important to wear a mask when using this powder - it is not to be breathed - it is very caustic. It can be used on any tissues that must be bagged and it is also useful when preparing decomposed bodies. A bead of glue along the suture line can help to assure that no leakage can occur.

There are also cases about bodies which had been dead or unattended for several days. These are called decomposed bodies (or de-comps). In such cases, the dead body begins to decay and just as the flesh becomes moist, the inner organs begin to liquify. It is difficult to remove such bodies since it is nearly impossible to find a point to grab for lifting. Wearing a filtered mask, we usually spread a double sheet on the ground and then gently scoot (or roll) the body onto it. We attempt to save any tissues which may have fallen from the body. The body is then taken to the autopsy laboratory, weighed and measured then placed in a "separate" cooler and held there until time for the autopsy. The cooler also tends to retard the continued putrefaction of the body so that the tissues will cease to decay and, thereby, the odors are lessened. When removing a de-comp, we must be fully garbed in protective plastic with gloves and masks - the masks have air filters. The odor is prominent and some removers initially use scented creams (or ammonia) placed on the upper lip, others smoke cigars to avoid the odors.

In the autopsy lab, we smock-up fully and we carefully lift the decomposed body onto the table. The procedure is essentially the same but with consideration that the tissues have turned to "mush." The (masked) pathologist will search the exterior of the body for evidence of trauma such as cutting or bruising. When the cavities are opened, all that is available is liquid. Small samples of the liquid from the skull and the liquid from the torso and abdomen are all saved for microscopic study. When the pathologist is finished, the remaining liquid is discarded; we use a few stitches to close the torso as much as possible then place the body in a plastic bag and return it to the de-comp cooler until the mortician can remove it. The mortician also has special procedures he employs in dealing with decomposed bodies. Discussion regarding the mortician's procedures will be described later.

One of the major aspects of the focus of the forensic autopsy aspect was the fact that the Forensic Pathologist was a key to the payment of insurance claims. I learned that if a case was finally classified as an "accident," as a result of the forensic examination, some insurance policies will pay double indemnity. So, as we examined our cases, which seemed to be suicides, an autopsy could clarify the actual cause of death for the insurance companies. The police appreciated it too.

During this period, I also experienced one of the worst things one could imagine (no, I wasn't locked in a cooler, no I wasn't stalled in traffic while transporting a de-comp . . .) at the beginning of the procedure, the doctor wanted to see the back of the body. I stood on a small stool which enabled me to reach completely across the body. I pulled the body over toward me and the point when the body was completely on its side, the stool slipped and I fell back and pulled the body off the table on top of me and we both hit the floor. I was trapped on the floor with a dead body lying on top of me. The doctor called in some help and they removed the

44

body and replaced it on the table. I never used that stool again! I was hoping that the doctor would not find head and facial injuries on that body which had occurred during this fall. Anyway, I realize that a forensic pathologist can determine the difference between a post-mortem injury and an injury which may have caused the death of this individual. I could have caused some post-mortem injuries with that fall.

Except for that incident (and one time finger cut), the autopsy room provided a fascinating experience and it interested me in the possibility of studying Forensic Science as a career. It is fortunate that we were required to have Hepatitis shots before working there. In the end, here was another chance to consider medical school. Unfortunately, I was unable to do that as I received a call, after three years in the autopsy lab, offering me a position in the career I had sought after the Air Force. The hiring freeze was removed and, in accepting that position, it required another major move, but it was significantly more lucrative. So again, I interrupted my drive for work in the mortuary, or related, business.

After I relocated to another city and began my new work, I took time to seek out the local mortuaries and forensic science labs for opportunities. As it turned out, my new career position required me to work rotating shifts and kept me from extra work in the autopsy lab. In my new work, I was sent to two other cities train. As a result, I became acquainted with more (Medical Examiners). I was pretty nosy.

\* \* \* \* \* \* \* \* \* \* \* \* \* \* \* \* \* \* \* \* \* \* \* \* \* \* \* \* \* \* \* \* \* \* \* \*

### Adage

Always remember that the mortician is your friend -
he is the last one to let you down

### and

A morticians job starts at the ground and he works his way down!

\* \* \* \* \* \* \* \* \* \* \* \* \* \* \* \* \* \* \* \* \* \* \* \* \* \* \* \* \* \* \* \* \* \* \* \*

# 4

**Disposition Methods (Alternatives to Burial)**

**Cremation**

The Cremation procedure arose from, perhaps 20,000 years ago with the Mungo Lady whose cremated remains were found at Mungo lake, Australia.

Evidence of cremation has been found in the Middle East. The Egyptians had banned cremation - notice the extensive embalming record begun by the Egyptians. The Babylonians, Persians and Phoenicians. The Greeks and Phoenicians practiced inhumation (burial). Cremation actually appeared at about the 12th Century BC - most of that influence was from Minor Asia. The Romans used both procedures. In Europe, cremation was evident in c2000 B.C. Most probably, the earliest form of cremation is from Homer's account of Patroclus' burial in a tumulus (L. small hill) where a body is buried and a mound of dirt and stones is placed over the grave.

Cremation is subject to religious approvals such as for Hinduism and Jainism which actually prescribe it. Jewish law forbids it.

In 1873, Professor Bruneti presented a cremation oven at the Vienna Exposition and in 1874, for the Cremation Society of Great Britain; that was followed by the first Crematoria which appeared in Europe (1874). In America, it was presented by Charles F. Winslow in Salt Lake City, Utah in 1877; many other countries followed. In the 19th Century, Sir Henry Thomas, physician to Queen Victoria, suggested that disposition by heat would serve to eliminate germs.

Cremation also had its periods of controversy such as during WWII when the Nazi concentration camps disposed of massive numbers of bodies through cremation. There was also the Tri-State Crematory Incident in 2002 where 334 corpses which were to have been cremated were found intact on the crematory grounds. The families had received ashes made-up of wood and cement dust. The owner had 387 charges filed against him and he received two 12-year prison sentences to be followed by 75 years probation after his incarceration.

Another incident was the 2004 Tsunami India Ocean Earthquake which killed an estimated 300,000 people. The identification of bodies was so difficult, the authorities decided to have mass cremation in order to avert disease which could affect the rest of the countrymen. One problem was that they separated the bodies into two groups - Westerners and Local Asians. In that process, Japan and Korea did not receive the bodies of their countrymen.

In America today, the process of cremation has improved over the years and cremation torts (ovens) have become very efficient. The standard ones are very effective, but, there are now "turbo" torts which create a double pass of the the flame with an afterburner to ensure the complete disintegration of the bones and elimination of most gases and other emanations. The standard retort (weighing 18 tons) costs approximately $35,000 and requires about 5-6 hours (3 hours in a turbo-retort) to complete a body (depending upon the body weight - it is calculated to be 1 hour per 99 lb. of body weight) and heats up to about 1500-1650 degrees F. At that temperature obliterates germs and viruses. There are also 6 sizes of retorts, the largest is used for large bodies (up to 385 Kilos = 848.7797 Lb). The turbo-retort has a special feature wherein the heat is deflected from exit and recycled to the burning area again before it exits. This also reduces the amount of time to consume a body. The smoke is cooled then is exhausted through the chimney. It is fueled by natural gas and propane. (In the early 1960's, coal and coke were used). Due to EPA regulations, crematories must be shut down before night-fall; this is in order to assure that nothing illegal is being burned at night). Also, in the past, older retorts were said to have a problem with escaping gasses and mercury in the exhausted smoke. The body contains sulphur, carbon, potassium, fat and water, therefore the effluence from the chimney is not zero - but, it is low.

The chamber of the 18 ton unit, holds only one body at a time (it is illegal to cremate more than body at a time) (An exception may occur when you have a mother and a stillborn child together). In cases where very large individuals (over 440 pounds) are to be cremated, it may be necessary to sever chunks of body fat so that he can fit - one problem is the factor of burning fat - if you have ever had a kitchen fire from lard or cooking oil, you can see the problem. In such cases, it would be good to have the fire department there to supervise the operation. Such large people may require two retorts with two separate firings to complete the job (both will require a container). There are now retorts built for oversized bodies.

Cases like that are not so common, so the funeral director has to determine whether he should purchase an oversized retort or share one with another mortuary.

It is necessary to remove all metals from the body before cremation. In addition, pacemakers must be removed. A magnet is passed through the cremains to locate any stray bits of metal. The inner bricks of a retort are made of aluminus silicate (aluminum-based sand material) - these are heat-resistant refractory bricks. It protects the metal parts of the oven and the binder chemicals inside. The body is in a container and it is either transported into the retort through a motorized feeding system or through manual means (with a pusher rod) and the body and container are inserted (charged). The person(s) involved must wear protective clothing and goggles and remain well away from the open door of the oven. After the door is closed, the retort starts; there is a blast of 1,500 degree flame which is aimed directly at the heart of the individual. Newer retorts have automatic shutoff switches in the event an emergency shutdown becomes necessary. The computer-operated retort will assure that the proper temperature has been reached - at that point, the door cannot be reopened. The refractory bricks should be replaced every 5 years.

At the end of the process, the door opens automatically; a short cool-down period is required and the operator removes the ashes with some special tools, such as a toothless rake, places the ashes with a push broom into a container (dust-pan-like) being careful to collect every grain of material from the retort. He then takes the collected remains into another room where he can run the magnet through the ashes and pick up and remove any remaining metal parts which may have survived (dental or orthopedic materials); the ashes are then put though a grinder (similar to a blender) to pulverize the large bony materials which may have remained. Typically, the scull and rib cage bones do not break down fully. The ashes are then packed into a 5 lb. cloth or plastic container - again with special care to collect **all** of ashes. He may have to tamp it down to assure that all the remains are securely in the container.

We have always called it ashes, but in reality, what remains is bone fragment. When all of this has been completed, the appropriate mortuary is called and its personnel will collect it and return it to the mortuary and, in turn, carefully (no loss of ash or bone), place them (tamping them) into a purchased cremation urn, present it for ceremonies or make personal delivery to the family. If they are unclaimed by the family, they are stored in the mortuary until final disposition is determined.

It would amaze you as to how many urns of ashes are never claimed by families (perhaps 30,000 per year). They remain stored in the mortuaries or they may be submitted for County burial in government-owned property as is done with unclaimed (intact) bodies.

When Sir Henry Thomas established that cremation obliterates germs and viruses, he cited the fact that in burials, there is decomposition and liquification which can seep into the ground and affect the water table (remember Egypt?). Fortunately, the Egyptians discovered that embalming cured that problem. Later, the idea of cremation was embraced as a more efficient and less-costly process. And today, because of government regulations, we know that there are minimal amounts of gases that escape into the air from crematoria - older models were found to emanate mercury fumes.

In today's world, people are always trying to save money and one way to do that is through the cremation process. For about $700 to $1,200, you can dispose of a body in a professional and legal manner. This a fraction of what you will pay for a full fledged casket funeral. Of course, the costs are variable according to the type of final urn selected for the ashes.

One may choose to have a funeral ceremony or a memorial service, but, overall, you will find that cremation is the most cost-efficient method of disposal. If you were to compare this to a funeral with a casket, viewing, church rite and you will find a significant difference in costs. Typically, bodies which are to be cremated are not embalmed since the final viewing is for the immediate family only. If the body is to be viewed by the public before cremation, an embalming will be performed as a means to protecting the health and safety of the public. The embalming process is a way to provide disinfection and preservation of the body. Most bodies are interred without a viewing and families tend to prefer the lesser cost of cremation.

Since the body is broken down into ashes, the only time there can be a viewing is by the immediate family before it is sent to the crematorium. This is to help to accommodate the closest family members only. The body is prepared in a brief manner with a gown or drape covering and some makeup on the face and hands, The body is dressed in a hospital gown-type of cover and placed on a rolling gurney and covered from the belt-line downward with a white sheet. The gurney is placed in a chapel or a slumber room for the viewing.

Most State laws require full preparation (embalming) of a body before it is exposed to public viewing - for the protection of public health. This process is meant to provides disinfection and preservation of the body. Viewings prior to cremation or a viewing for identification purposes is to allow the family to have a final good-bye period - such cases do not require embalming. An embalming before a viewing incurs additional costs.

While burial, cremation and entombment are, by far, the most preferred method of body disposal, there are also a few other techniques which have emerged and which may be requested by a family. Here are a few examples of some alternate (perhaps unorthodox) methods of disposal:

Alkaline Hydrolysis - involves the use of lye to dissolve tissues and the remaining material can be scattered, buried or even sent down a drain. (Also called resomation)

Mummification - used in cases where permanent storage is desired. There are people who are licensed to do this process of dehydration.

Cryopreservation - this is a process where cells or entire tissues are preserved through cooling to sub-zero temperatures (-196 degrees C) - the boiling point of nitrogen. It requires that cryoprotectant solutions be used to avoid damage to the sells due to freezing and thawing. It is purported that this will provide an indefinite longevity for the cells. It has been difficult to prove. The ultra-cold temperatures of -321F is required for successful preservation of complex biological structures.

There are many risks to consider with this process, such as: The effects of certain solutions, extracelluar ice formation, dehydration and intracellular ice formation. This process is best for smaller units   of cells such as for semen, and blood - not an entire body.

Other terms and distinctions:

Cryobiology - the study of low temperature on organisms

Cryosurgery - the use of low temperatures in surgery to freeze and destroy malignant tissues.

Cryonics -the cryopdreservation of humans with the intent of future revival.

Cryoelectronics - research involving superconductivity at low temperatures.

Cryotronics - the practical application of cryoelectronics.

Plastination - a technique to preserve bodies or body parts. It was developed by Gunther Von Hagens (1977). Water and fats are replaced by plastics - the result is specimen that retain its original shape.

Promession- A form of burial in which human remains are disposed of by freeze-drying. Invented by Swedish Biologist Susanne Wigh Masak. Promession is derived from the Italian word for "promise."

Burial at Sea - the disposal of human remains in the ocean which is regularly done by navies and by private citizens in many countries.

Cannibalism - this one is not recommended, and we do not use it in this country, but, it still occurs in many societies of the world. It is also called anthropophagy. (While this technique is not recommended for members of our society, it is certainly a way to dispose of bodies.

Space Shots - Was it Timothy Leary who had his ashes shot into space?

Sky Exposure - see the Tibetan and Parsi Towers of Silence. The body is placed upon a high wooden man-made tower and it is decomposed naturally.

Taxidermy - Yes, there are actually people who offer this service for the "forever" preservation of humans.

Emergency Common Burial - this is used when a large number of bodies have resulted from a natural disaster.

Freeze-Dry Process - this is a form of progressive dehydration wherein the body is placed into a chamber where all water is removed very slowly.

This allows the tissues to maintain their shapes. Everyone has the experience when their fingers have been soaking in water for a while the fingers appear to become withered. This process is the opposite approach but with same effect. As the water content of the body Is reduced and leaves the internal normal body, dehydrations occurs and the body will slowly dry out and with no withering. With this new process the very slow removal of the water in the cells allows the skin to retain its original shape. In the end, you have a fully formed body which weighs one-tenth its former weight. It can be painted to appear dressed and have a professional application of make-up which it will make it appear to look normal - yet - preserved forever.

This is similar to some of the other methods which allow the body to be retained (not buried, burned nor decayed) forever. (Also called promession).

Donation to Science - A popular practice is to have one's body donated for use in hospitals or universities. Such bodies are use to teach detailed anatomy to medical students. In some cases, there is a need for bone marrow. If a donated body is available, there are crews which will dissect the total body and remove the long bones - such as the femur, humerus, tibia, fibula, radius and ulna. After the bones have been removed, pvc pipe is used to replace them. The ilia is connected to the patella with pipe, then the lower long bones are replaced with more pipe. The missing empty areas around the piles are replaced with cotton and the edges of the skin is sewn back together. This simulates the full size of the body. In other cases, they remove so much bone that the reconstruction won't work, so, they place all the remains in a plastic bag, box it up and send took a mortuary for cremation. At the mortuary, we use bottles of formaldehyde and embalming powder on the tissues and seal the bag. We then consult the family to determine final disposition; usually submit it for cremation. If there is no immediate family, we submit the remains for county burial.

Some of these methods are rather exotic and will cost you, perhaps, more than a typical burial service wherein you determine what you want done and you can personalize your desires and purchase the services as a package. As you can see, there are myriad choices when it comes to body disposal. Most people in this country are opting for cremation since it is less costly than a burial.

\* \* \* \* \* \* \* \* \* \* \* \* \* \* \* \* \* \* \* \* \* \* \* \* \* \* \* \* \* \* \* \* \*

## How much can you bear?

I was called one evening to make a removal at an accident scene. I met my partner who had secured the van from the mortuary. It was a collision at an intersection with a van and a small motorcycle. Some people had gathered from throughout the neighborhood. As we approached the scene, we found a person lying in the street. He was wearing a bear costume. He was on his way to a Halloween party and had made a turn and drove in front of a van at a stop sign. He was wearing the bear head which had restricted his vision.

When I returned, I was about to tell my wife about it, but, she greeted me with a hose and thoroughly soaked me down. She said that she was going to do this every time I returned from a removal.

\* \* \* \* \* \* \* \* \* \* \* \* \* \* \* \* \* \* \* \* \* \* \* \* \* \* \* \* \* \* \* \* \*

# 5

## Religious/Cultural Considerations

Another concern would be the consideration of the religious preferences of the diseased. As you have seen, the history of processes and rites regarding the final services has experienced many changes over time. However, historical roots can be seen in the various techniques from which to choose. Of course, in consideration of the number of cultures and religions, I can only give a few examples of certain ritual needs which the modern mortician will have to serve. This type of information is part of a morticians schooling. Every mortician will do his/her best to follow the wishes of the family and do all he can to follow and religious rites which may be involved.

Christian Burial - this is burial of a deceased person with Christian Ecclesiastical rites is to be in consecrated ground. Historically, Christians generally were opposed to cremation and inhumation was the preferred method. More recently, however, there has been reduced opposition among Protestants. Even Catholics accept cremation - only the Eastern Orthodox churches forbid it for the most part. Christians believe that death still inflicts pain, nevertheless, we will not have to fight death forever, for if we are **in Christ**, we need not fear death. We will have victory over death and its effects.

> Immanuel Kant, 18th Century philosopher said: "If we don't believe
> in the afterlife, this life has been meaningless."

Greeks and Romans practiced cremation. The Jews preferred burial (and they still do). The Christians separated the mortal/physical aspect of the human body from the soul. The primary concern was the departing of the soul from this life into eternal life was paramount. The religious aspect also called for a dignified religious service/ceremony. It begins with a 'wake' derived from a Jewish custom which called for a vigil with the remains with prayer and singing of psalms.

Next was Absolution involved the laying of an etched cross was a typical procedure. The Offertory was also a time when attendees were given the opportunity to offer monetary gifts. Catholics may have a 'Mass for the Dead.' After that a graveside service can be held where there are prayers and sprinkling of the casket.

In Japan, a country with almost 100% cremations - some areas ban burials. Cremation rose rapidly after WWII, but, mostly for the rich. A traditional Japanese funeral consists of a wake, cremation, burial in a family grave and a memorial service. Funerals in japan are very costly due to the scarcity of burial plots. The scattering of ashes has become more popular.

In Japan, the funeral is accompanied with Buddhist rituals. The deceased is given a Buddhist name - in this way, they are prevented from returning if their name is called. At the service, the family will place flowers and around the head. The casket is taken to a crematory where the family will witness the loading of the casket into the retort. They will wait through the burning period to receive the cremains. The family will actually participate in separating the bone from the ashes with large chop sticks. They will attempt to identify bones and carefully place them in the urn with the feet and leg bones first and the head last (on top). The ashes are placed in other containers and divided among the family members. The main urn is placed on a altar in the home for 35 days before it is taken to the family grave.

In some case, they use professional dressers who provide a formal dressing of the body while the family observes. American funeral directors will attempt to provide as much of the Japanese ceremony into his funeral as possible.

For Chinese deceased, we realize that funeral customs are very important. Because of the various locations from which they derive. Inhumations are very common. The family members will wear mourning clothes made of five different materials according to how close the relationship was to the deceased. This is called the '5-rank sable.' The funeral is held in the one which has been decorated with scrolls and other hangings. Family and friends may visit for a 7-day period. Taoists are invited to chant scriptures to release them from purgatory. After the burial, the offspring shall guard the tomb a day and a half; this is called 'to observe mourning.' Other than inhumation, they also use water burial, open burial and a technique they call the 'hanging coffin burial.' Again, American embalmers will attempt to observe as many conditions of the culture as possible.

Jewish Services - Jewish tradition requires that the deceased should not be unattended; a Shormer (watchman), selected by the family, stays with the body from the time of the death until the funeral is held. Members of the family might also stay. A relative (spouse, parent, sibling or child) may be assigned as a mourner. Other family members may observe. The mourner's (Onen's) primary obligation is to coordinate the arrangement of a proper Jewish burial of the deceased. The Rabbi is the first one to be called; with him, the time for the services in coordination with the family is established and scheduled. The service may be held in the Temple, the Synagogue or even at the cemetery.

Jewish tradition calls for the burial to occur as soon as possible after death. It is most respectful if the burial can occur without any delay. Jewish tradition says that you must not look at a person who cannot look back, it is seen as disrespectful; therefore, there is no viewing by visitors. The mortician would present a closed-casket funeral service. Embalming of the body will not be done unless the State requires it. A sacred society may be contacted to perform the necessary functions. They will perform the Tahrah (purification), bathe and dress the deceased in Tachrichim Shrouds (burial garments) - Men will prepare men and women will prepare women. The shroud is a simple garment without pockets. The represents the fact that we take nothing with us - God judges us on our merits, not according to any wealth we have amassed. Tradition calls for a wooden casket with no metal parts; that may range from a simple unfinished pine box to a sold walnut plank and which was not built on the Sabbath. (There are other casket requirements and these are described later in this book). There will be no flowers (however, a Rabbi may approve of a small floral tribute to be placed on the casket). The service may last about twenty minutes and consist of a recitation of Psalms, Scripture Readings and a Eulogy. The mourners may participate in a rendering of the garment with a tear or a black ribbon - it is symbolic of the tear in the mourner's heart. If the deceased is a parent, the ribbon will be placed on the left side - for others, it will be placed on the right side.

Everyone will accompany the deceased to the properly selected burial site. After the casket has been lowered and the grave is filled (attendees may participate by tossing some dirt into the grave), the Kaddish prayer is said.

In some parts of the country there have been instances where the body/casket is entombed in a mausoleum (above-ground burial) - apparently with the permission of the Rabbi. After the burial, the attendees form a Shura - a double line facing each other forming a pathway through which the family members and the mourners may pass. After this, the attendees may express their condolences. Again, with a little knowledge of certain requirements, the mortician can provide a proper and meaningful service.

Of course, there are many more religions to be considered and its procedures understood.  This is one of the subjects  which will be learned at a certified Mortuary school or College.

# 6

## A New Mortuary School?

An offer to study for a higher education degree caused me to relocate again and that set the stage for another effort to get involved in forensic pathology and the mortuary business. At my new location, I again sought to locate part-time work in the death business. I located a mortuary which hired me as a 'remover' - I was to be on-call to remove bodies (after hours and weekends); I would be sent to various hospitals, nursing homes, and accident scenes to remove bodies and return them to the mortuary or to the medical examiner's office. This was another opportunity to work in a mortuary and learn more about the business. I was again told that I would have to attend a mortuary embalming school in order to get licensed to work as a funeral director. By this time, the age clock was working against me and because of all the formal administrative training I had completed, I wondered whether I, myself, could develop an embalming school in my own town and eliminate the need to go to another State so as to train. And so it began - my efforts to create an embalming school.

I contacted an associate who was a Dean at a local Community College. I told him of my plan and he immediately became interested. He told me of a nearby Air Force Base that had closed and that some buildings were available for sale. He began the process to determine whether he could get his college to obtain one of the buildings and use it to develop my idea. I visited some of the buildings that were to be made available to assure that we could meet the standards of a mortuary school, i.e. it requires space for offices, classrooms, casket room, storage, space for a prep room, a garage and a chapel. After we determined which building would work best, I took measurements of the overall building and proceeded to design a floor plan which could be used for our purposes. I also contacted the National Funeral Directors Association (NFDA) - the national organization which oversees all the Mortuary Schools in the country. From them, I obtained all the legal requirements and procedures for the development of a school. I had to coordinate with all State, County and City entities. In addition, all other mortuaries were contacted in the State and local area to seek their support.

The plan was to provide an accredited college program which would offer an

Associate in Arts Degree with a major in Mortuary Science. In addition, it would be a center for the offering of continuous educational workshops for anyone working in mortuaries (local and nationwide). I coordinated with the Medical Examiners Office to obtain approval to access unclaimed bodies which could be used for student embalming training. Those bodies were from their unclaimed roster or those designated for county burial. It was a long process, but, the school opened and, eventually, graduated many students. My coordination with the mortuaries throughout the State offered students the opportunity to have some on-the- job training while in school. A curriculum was developed and coordinated with the college, and the NFDA; a building was acquired and prepared for the remodeling process. The only thing left was to get accredited by the NFDA and the college. Finally, it became a reality and since, has had many graduates.

In this process, it was necessary to work closely with the National Funeral Director's Association (NFDA). This caused us (my wife and me) to attend National Conventions in various cities. My wife was surprised when she entered a large convention center room with "acres" of space where one could see all the paraphernalia used by funeral directors everywhere. There were hearses (funeral coaches), caskets and all the possible adornments, displays with lotions, funeral home building information (floor plans), videos of products of all sorts, clothing, urns and more.

We also attended convention break-outclasses on various aspects of funeral work. I wanted to attend a class on restorative art - when we arrived at the classroom, it was very full and that forced us to sit in the front row. My wife was faced with large-screen photos of horrible accidents and the required facial repairs and how they were attended. She was hoping that was the last the we would be late for a session. On the convention floor, we were given many samples to take home. My wife gathered an assortment of lotions, thinking they would make nice gifts for our friends. When we returned to the hotel room she unpacked her "goody-bag" and then noticed that all the lotion bottles had names of funeral companies printed on them - so much for gifts.

The Mortuary College curriculum was developed from the NFDA Standards and included courses such as: * Introduction to Funeral Service, Embalming Theory and Lab Experiences, Funeral Merchandising, Mortuary Law, Pathology, Thanato-Microbiology, Pathology, Restorative Art, Funeral Directing and Counseling, Thanatochemistry, National Board Exam Review, and Internship.

(*Other variations can be offered such as: Morals and Ethics, Motivation, Grief, Managing Stress, Hazardous Chemicals and Toxic Substances, The Funeral Rule Compliance, Preplanning, Grief, Sensitivity, Communicable Disease, Universal Precautions, Job Burnout, Pre-need Funerals/Insurance, Accounting, Marketing, etc. As one can see, the breadth of knowledge is evident inasmuch as funeral directors want to offer the best services they can possibly deliver.

The schooling is typically 2 years and the student emerges with an A.A Degree (if the school is affiliated with an institution for higher learning). There are also private Mortuary Colleges which offer a Certificate of Completion. One very important aspect is the preparation for the State and/or national Board Exam which allows the person to legally function in the business.

Every college class has a prefix, so I was seeking an appropriate prefix for our courses. A natural choice seemed to be FUN (for funeral). We settled for MS (mortuary Science). Someone might have congered a motto such as , "We put the FUN into Funeral Director training." I couldn't let hat happen

**Other Skills**

During all this school-development, I experienced some additional training at my local mortuary where I had been hired as a remover. I wanted to branch out and learn more of the funeral skills which would later be required. In one instance, I had an expert there teach me all about the make-up (farding) process to make a person presentable. While learning that, we received cases where people had been disfigured in the head and face. As an art major and a sculptor, I became even further enthralled with this process. We could make people presentable in a casket, even though they had had severe head trauma. (Notice, I said, "presentable," not "perfect.") My trainer spent hours with me on repairing facial injuries (this is a process which is not on the fees list). In most cases, where a trauma had been incurred, he would take more time to repair the face and head than he took to initially embalm the body. This is the reason many mortuaries will not agree to repair a body to be presentable for viewing - it is time-consuming and no fee is chargeable except that it falls under the category of "Professional Services," which usually means only embalming. In my training, we had some dismembered parts to consider as well; in those cases, the parts had to be embalmed separately. There were times when we used a form of chicken wire and lots of embalming wax to complete repairs. In one case, a young girl had sustained loss of the right side of her face in a traffic accident, we used wires and cotton stuffing and rebuilt the cheek bone and the eye socket. We created an eyelid from some of her own skin (usually from leg) and added some hair from the back of the head to make an eyelash. After final application of mortician's wax, the make-up was applied and the girl became presentable in her casket.

During this period, I refined my embalming technique to the point where I could do it without supervision. I was able to do this since I now had an "Apprentice License." I still had to attend an embalming school to complete my formal education and pass the National and State Board Examinations as a funeral director. All graduates are required to take the National Board Exams, however not all States have a State Board Examination. Formerly, the apprenticeship preceded formal schooling, now, the apprenticeship follows graduation from an embalming school.

Final Preparation - Make-up

At the end of the embalming process, the body had to become ready for the presentation to the family. This means that we had to use makeup to make the face and hands presentable (farding). One has to consider the fact that the skin begins to decompose immediately after death. Decomposition is evident in the appearance of longer nails or hair. The idea that the hair and the nails will continue to grow after death is a myth. It is, rather, a function of the dehydration process as the skin dries and withdraws from certain areas. A body that is severely decomposed will not be shown to anyone.

In a typical death case, the skin softens and becomes more difficult to apply makeup. Although the law does not require embalming or the need for cosmetizing, it does require it, except where there is to be a public viewing (this is for the protection public health). A cursory makeup of the face and hands is a good thing to do if the immediate family (only) wants to view the body or there is a question as to the identification of the individual. In the latter event anyone with valid interest my view him. Many mortuaries and Medical Examiners offices had small windowed rooms for this purpose. This assures that there is no contact with the body by the general public and the requirement to restrict or deny exposure to the body to the public is preserved.

After all the restorative work has been completed, the makeup process begins. The list of general supplies need for accomplishing a good makeup job might include:

 The make-up is available from such companies as, (Graftobian Make-Up Co. and others):  (General household makeup can also be used, however, it probably will not have the staying effect which is referred in the preparation of a dead body).  It can also used for 'touch-up.'
   Make-up kit supplies:

>    Adhesives and adhesive removers
>    Air Brush makeup
>    Cosmetizing Creme Foundations
>    Cosmetizing Kit
>    Cosmetizing Modeling Wax (Morticians wax will be fine)
>    Eye and Lip-lining pencils
>    Facial Powders
>    Lining Shades and Concealers
>    Lip color cups and Stacks
>    Miscellaneous Tools and Containers
>    Pressed Powder Brush
>    Pressed Powder Foundations
>    Rouges Highlighters and Concealers
>    Setting Spray
>    A box to hold all of the cosmetic materials

The skin of a deceased person feels different due to the dehydration process. We begin with a gentle scrubbing of the face with a hand wash (soap).  While scrubbing, special attention is paid to locate any trauma wounds or cuts and bruises. We pay close attention to those areas).  There may be areas which have been rubbed by pavement or other objects; care is taken not to rub too hard or use an overly course sponge - it may have been necessary to repair areas where the skin has been rubbed off.  Morticians' wax is used to prepare those aspects which may draw attention.  Mortician's Wax is a great product which is flesh-colored and it has a malleable consistency so that it can be formed to create any type of skin formation the mortician seeks.  It can also be tinted to match color areas.

The cosmetizer must be certain to check photo(s) in the event a scar or defect was a part of the deceased appearance during his/her life - it should be as accurate as possible). It is also necessary to make certain that the male cadavers are clean-shaven (except for their mustaches or beards). The skin will develop brown spots where post-mortem bleeding has occurred from the shave. That also has to be covered with wax or makeup. If a mustache was inadvertently shaven off, another one has to be fabricated using hair from the back of the head. The next step was the application of a base material to create a good working surface for the makeup - it is called Glow Tint which appears brownish-orange in color.

It is a liquid which can be brushed on the face and hands. This is important because it allows cadaver makeup to be applied easier. Cadaver makeup is thicker than most makeup used in theater work but it can be thinned with massage cream or a product called dry wash. The thicker makeup can help to hide unwanted creases in the skin (it can be tinted to personal requirements). One must be careful to assure that the final color is consistent with the color of the other skin parts and to a natural color as may be shown in the photograph which was being used. (Hopefully it is not too old - in many cases you will receive a photograph of the deceased from his/her younger years -ouch!!). Just take a look at the obituaries.

Many embalmers prefer to use wax on the lips since the effect of dehydration can be very evident in the lips, however a massage cream or a humectant (a substance that promotes the retention of moisture) can be used. Without this, the lips will tend to part and will require repair (hopefully, not during the funeral service). The lips have been glued shut and it can hold for a limited time. Dehydration is the worst enemy, especially when there is a prolonged period of time between preparation of the body and the funeral. The outer orifices are stuffed with cotton to prevent flies or insects to enter the body. Cotton is stuffed into the nose and ears and, sometimes, the mouth for that reason. We wouldn't want maggots to appear at the wrong time.

Massaging cream is useful to keep the skin looking good. The makeup job is concluded with the application of rouge, mascara and lipstick (a check with the family before you selection of the lipstick color is probably wise - the family might want to have a certain color used. The male face is somewhat easier to detail since men, typically, do not wear makeup. In most case, the Glo-Tint is adequate). (However, the male cadaver has to be shaved carefully!)

Dressing of the body takes a special skill since the body is lying prone and is, perhaps, too heavy to lift. In some cases, a mortician will cut the garments (shirt and jacket) down the back and then dress the body one half at a time. (Remember the spit clothes?) To do that the body has to be rolled onto one side (on its shoulder, while the garment is sleeved over the arm and placed under the midpoint of where the body is lying. The body is then rolled back to its lying state and then rolled the other way to dress the other side. When the body is returned to its natural lying state; the trousers are put on in the normal manner and the mortician and his helper raise the legs (which are stiff), pull it under the buttocks and placed in the proper position. The shirt is tucked, belt is buckled, the jacket is positioned properly and the only thing left is the necktie (and any jewelry the family wishes to leave on the body..

The tying of a necktie sounds easy, however, many people have difficulty tying a necktie onto someone else. One technique (the easiest) is where the mortician places the tie around his own neck and makes the knot. The tie remains loose enough to remove it over his head - he then places it over the cadaver's head and in the proper position where it merely needs to be cinched up. Another dressing technique is where the shirt and jacket remain in tact and the body can be dressed simply by the rolling over of the body to each side.

This process may be difficult because the neck will typically be enlarged or swollen, due to the embalming process or, especially if the person had had CPR a the time of death. This can be reduced if the embalmer squeezes the neck or uses a specially-formed sand bag while embalming.

There is one more technique which can be used and also does not require cutting of the garments. The shirt and jacket (separately) are set down in the normal position. The garment is then gathered up to the neck until it forms a sort-of tube of cloth. It is then pulled down to the stomach of the deceased where the hands and arms can be directed into the sleeve holes (remember, the arms are not flexible at this point). The body is raised at the shoulders and the garments is then pulled up and over the head and then pulled under the body and manipulated into position. This is very difficult if the deceased is a very large person. I remember the first time I saw split clothing and wondered what that was all about - now, it is all beginning to make some sense to me. Now, dressing a body is not as difficult as I once had thought. I didn't see any cases where we cut the clothing before dressing. That catalogue I had once seen as a youngster had told me lots of things which I finally understood when I actually encountered them.

Caskets

The next step is to load the body into a casket or a cremation container. If the body is very small, it can be done by one person. Most mortuaries are equipped with a small crane (on wheels) and several support straps which can be used by one person to transfer a body. More typically there will be two to three 'lifters.' The lifters will stand side-by-side on one side of the table and cradle their arms under the body and, together supporting the entire body, lift the body and, without a lot of steps, rotate themselves from a dressing table to a casket or container. Once the body is lowered into the casket, the mortician will make adjustments to assure that the head and pillow are properly in place (clear of the lid) and the arms and hands are positioned in repose and that the clothes are adjusted to look proper. The two parts of the casket lid will be nearly closed (making certain that the lid does not touch the face). For a casket which opens as a full lid (a full-couch casket), the lid will be held partially open until final adjustments are made just prior to the service. The body in the casket and on a bier will either be wheeled into the chapel or to a visitation (slumber) room.

> Side Note: There are many types of caskets available and several
> are on display at the mortuary in the showroom. There
> are also catalogues from which to order specialty caskets
> or caskets that are not in the showroom,

One may select from caskets made of wood or metal. Wood is the oldest of all materials ever used for this purpose. Plywood and composite wood are used in some instances, but, it is the hard woods that are stronger and shock-resistant. As a renewable element, hardwood leaves a legacy for the following generations. Hardwoods come from leaf-bearing trees (deciduous). Hardwoods of this type do not necessarily have a hard surface. Most premium hardwood timber is grown on the eastern seaboard, e.g. Vermont, New Hampshire, Maine and Pennsylvania. There are 9,000 species of hardwoods of which, perhaps 4,000 are useful for manufacturing purposes. Hardwoods are of two types - open grain (oak and ash) and closed grain maple and poplar).The hardwoods that are most popular for caskets are the Premium Hardwoods such as Cherry, Mahogany and Walnut. Oak, Ash, Elm and Maple are Standard Hardwoods. The most common hardwoods are Poplar and Cottonwood.

A high quality casket is hand-molded and is hand-rubbed between multiple coats of lacquer. They are finished with a hand-rubbed polish with a high gloss or satin finish. Some wooden caskets are made without metal parts so as to be cremated. In these cases, people tend to purchase the lower-priced caskets. If an expensive cherry or mahogany wood casket is to be cremated, the mortician will scratch the surface and severely mar the casket so as to prevent recycling (resale) of the casket. The crematory manager will also be notified that such a casket is coming so he can watch out for metal parts and during and after the cremation. A better option might be a cherry veneer.

Since caskets evolved from its earliest days when they were built by furniture and cabinet makers, these types of workers still apply their knowledge to a wide variety of exterior finishes that will accent the grain patterns unique to each species of wood.

Caskets used for a Jewish (Orthodox) ceremony must have certain elements in it to be considered Kosher, such as:

A plain and simple casket is to be used to reaffirm that we are all equal in death.

Wooden dowels are used instead of nails and screws.

Any glue used must be vegetable-based - not animal-based.

The casket is to be made entirely of wood (with holes in the bottom or spaced wooden slats) to hasten decomposition.

The casket cannot be made on the Sabbath.

Interiors must be bio-degradable.

The bed of the casket must not be adjustable. A bed of 'wool-wool' (a large mattress) made of strands of wool is to be used.

Metal handles must be easily removable.

A Rabbi is available for consultation.

Metal Caskets

For thousands of years, artisans and craftsmen have adored the beauty of bronze and copper since they are the most durable of all metals. In 1963, caskets began to be made in bronze and copper. In more modern times, Stainless Steel and Carbon Steel have been made and have become more affordable to a greater segment of the population. These are made in a variety colors, trimmings and thicknesses ranging form 16 gauge (thick) and 20 gauge (thin).

(Remember, the higher the gauge, the thinner the metal. If you were to consider a one inch space, the one inch would represent 1 Gauge. If you filled the space with two pieces, that would be 2 gauge. The more pieces you split the parts into, the higher the gauge). Therefore, a 16 gauge piece of metal is thicker than a 20 gauge piece of metal). So, watch out when an automobile salesman tries to impress you with a certain gauge - remember when the foreign car salesmen tried to impress me with his praise of the gauge number of the metal used in his car - I replied that we could get a caskets thicker than that!

In the casket-making business, there are only 6 stamping companies that supply every casket maker. In some cases, a metal casket can be produced for $64 and they wholesale to the funeral director for $264. At the funeral home, the customer will pay $1,795 to $2,695. The difference between a 20 gauge and a 16 gauge is about $1,000. The highest priced casket is probably the bronze and copper listed as 32 oz or 34oz (wt per sq ft) range from $15,000 to $70,000 - they hold up very well - talk about snob appeal! You must be careful, ,however, you may have misled when you purchased a thin metal which will deteriorate easily.

Stainless steel is another popular material for caskets. It is referred to as a "semiprecious metal," (This is merely to differentiate it from other metal casket materials. This is a very durable material, but you must be aware that the bottoms of these caskets may be made of another material which might deteriorate readily. Expect to pay *$3,000 and up (depending upon your location).

Some caskets are called "sealers." These have rubber gaskets around the lid to provide 'protection' from the outside elements. With a sealer casket, the body will experience putrefaction (rotting) rather than dehydration. We have seen both of these with exhumed bodies.

Some people consider the purchase a casket from a source other a funeral director.

In the past, some mortuaries would wrap the cost of the casket into the overall costs and were found to be charging 300-700% markups. Now, because of the "Funeral Rule," which requires itemized pricing, that practice has stopped. If you provide a casket for a funereal service, beware that you aren't paying a 'handling charge.' There are some states (Louisiana, Virginia and Oklahoma) require the casket to be purchased from a mortician. If you prefer to purchase a separate casket, be prepared to have problems.

You have seen movies of the 'old west' where caskets were pine boxes with a wide upper and narrower part. These are referred to as "toe-pinchers," so, when people say, "Just put me in a pine box" - this is what they probably mean.

Urns

Throughout history, the remains of deceased loved ones have been handled in various ways. Traditional religious beliefs of the family were the general guideline. At first, it ranged from crude graves to elaborate tombs; late, as, cremation began to become acceptable, burial urns were introduced as a way to contain the cremated ashes.

The practice of burning a body to ashes is an old technique, however, it nearly came to a halt when Christians objected since they wanted to have the body buried in the traditional manner. But then, health concerns arose as a result of epidemic problems such as the plague. From that time forward, cremation began to be accepted as a normal procedure for the disposal of a dead human body. The Christians were able to justify the practice through various scriptural guidance. The Chinese had a strong belief in preservation of the body for the afterlife. They also believed in placing valuable materials in the coffin at the service. They developed an alternative method wherein a large funeral urn was used for the body which was then anatomically arranged and then placed in tombs.

As you approach this aspect of life and you lose a loved one and you opt for cremation, you must then consider the type of urn (another cost item) to be used for the cremains. Urns come in various styles, design and price ranges. Here are some examples of the range of prices you will need to consider: (prices can also vary according to location in the country).

Small marble urn vaults *$40-$175;
Grecian Marble urn* $25-$175
Medium Classic marble urns *$40-$250; Keepsake Marble urns
  *$60 - $120
Burial Containers  *$110-$550

Morticians are able to divide the ashes into as many parts as one desires so that family members might have a share of them. These may be placed inside of ornate sculptures which may contain as little as 1-2 teaspoons of ashes. They might also be small wooden boxes - it depends upon how many will participate in the division of the ashes. In addition, all or part of the ashes may be given to a family for scattering (in legal [laces) - and, of course, their budget.

In preparation for the general service, the chapel will be staged with the flowers and gifts and will be arranged to present a pleasing sight, the lights are set to present the mood and soft music is played on an in-house stereo. Just before the service is to begin, the casket lid will be raised and the clothing, pillow and hands are set in final position, the family is greeted and given time to spend with their deceased loved one. If they request adjustments (in the clothing or make-up), those can be completed before other people are admitted into the chapel. A cleric or religious representative will be greeted and admitted into the chapel where he/she can greet the family.

After the service, guests are escorted out - the family may want to remain until the casket is closed and sealed. The flowers are loaded into a separate flower car and transported to the cemetery.

Before funereal rites have been celebrated, the family must have purchased a final resting place. In our society, a burial or entombment is required as a place for disposition of dead human remains. Here are some reasons for it: it provides for a respectful handling of human remains, it brings closure for the family of the deceased; some consider it as a place from which to enter the afterlife, and it serves as a means of preventing odors.

This process requires some preliminary planning when arranging the funeral with a funeral director. You are actually purchasing a plot of land (like the property where you house sits). The cemetery costs will be separate from the cost of the funeral. A cemetery is to be selected; a fee for 'opening' and 'closing' of the grave;

a fee for the cement vault which covers the casket (for protection).  The cost for digging out and refilling the grave is a normal expectation.  Cemeteries usually require a vault (outside burial container).  These are made of concrete, steel or fiberglass; they look like box-covers and fit over a concrete slab which is first placed at the bottom of the grave - this acts as a 'floor' for the vault and provides some degree of protection from moisture.  The vault also prevents sinking of the ground over the casket which, without a vault will disintegrate and crash into itself leaving a distinct depression in the grass over the grave.  The lawn mowers will also appreciate a flat surface for mowing over the grave  The installation of the vault will incur another cost (about *$300).  We must remember that regardless of all the 'protective' measures we take, the body will still decompose over time.

Mausoleums are above-ground buildings where caskets are entombed in a sealed drawer-like chamber.  This is place for people who feel that they prefer to be buried above the ground and they present a pleasant area in the cemetery for visitation.  A sealed casket is preferred here since there is always the possibility of fluids escaping as the body dehydrates.

*all prices vary between place to place and from time to time.

Another option is a Columbarium, which is miniature version of the mausoleum where the cremains can be retained.  These are significantly priced less than a mausoleum space.

Another cost will be labeled a "Perpetual Care."  These funds allow for it to have continuous maintenance and upkeep of a cemetery  (%-15%).  You may have seen the results where cemeteries have not been maintained.  Here are some tips to consider as you approach this need:

> Get a printed itemized price list for everything you are considering buying. b
>
> Get a copy of the Cemetery's rules and regulations.
>
> Ask what types and sizes of monuments are approved?
>
> Ask what are the approved decorations - many will not accept
>     pinwheels and fences and most will not allow any glass decorations.

Ask if the cemetery site create transportation problems for you?

If you can't get the items you prefer, you might want to rethink you choice of that cemetery.

If you purchase too early and you change your mind, will you be able to resell it later?

Since land availability is decreasing, would it be smart to purchase a gravesite early?

Purchase cost of a gravesite varies. For a site in a rural area, consider the cost to be from *$200-$500. For urban areas, you might expect to pay from *$5,000 to **$10,000. To bury a burial urn, you can expect to pay about *$800.

In other cases, a body might require shipping to another city for its burial services. The process is similar to the previous one where the deceased is loaded into a casket then the casket is wrapped in heavy plastic and taped securely (for leak protection) and placed into a shipping container; the proper identification papers is secured with the casket (in the Memorial Record Tube) and the top is nailed shut. The container is wrapped with heavy cardboard. Metal straps are then wrapped around the outer container and connected tightly. The shipping paperwork is adhered to the lid and the box is transported to the cargo department at the airport where it is placed with other cargo scheduled for a flight which was prearranged by the mortuary. The shipment and the body are coordinated with the airline through a paper trail and the information with the casket (along with copies of the shipping documents) are attached for the receiving mortician; paperwork is signed and stamped and control of the shipment is in the hands of the airline. This sounds like a simple process, but, when combined with all the activities which accompany the preparation of several bodies, it can be quite challenging.

While most shipments are done in this way, (using a plywood outer container), there are also sealed metal cases which act as temporary caskets (Ziegler Case). These are sealed and the protect against leakage which might occur in transit.

71

\* \* \* \* \* \* \* \* \* \* \* \* \* \* \* \* \* \* \* \* \* \* \* \* \* \* \* \* \*

**Let's get this straight!**

It was a small service for family members only.  They were very traditional and wanted to provide a proper send-off for their loved one.  The elders wanted to be very precise and were somewhat at odds regarding the steps to be taken.

At the gravesite, it began: the elders couldn't agree on the position method of burial at the gravesite.  Because of tradition, we were to start the casket down slowly and stop it briefly when it was level to the grass line.  As we determined that it was level, one of the elders didn't agree and began to yell, "Flush it!, Flush it!

\* \* \* \* \* \* \* \* \* \* \* \* \* \* \* \* \* \* \* \* \* \* \* \* \* \* \* \* \*

# 7

## Mortuary Humor

As in any business, there are humorous incidents which occur. Throughout this book, I have shared some humorous circumstances we have had during my time as a mortuary apprentice. It is probably hard to believe, but, humor also occurs in the world of 'thanatology.' I have a wife who is not thrilled by my fascination with the death process and she avoids any contact with it whenever possible. Unfortunately, she is stuck with me and occasionally became involved in my 'side-job.' I did know, however, that she had a little nervous curiosity in what happens at the mortuary. Thus, the purpose of this book is to inform and enlighten those who have that type of curiosity about the functions of morticians and personnel in other aspects of the processes which take place after a death. Recently, it has become possible to consult the internet and witness some of the very operations that are described in this book.

The humor does not reflect any disrespect to the deceased. They are usually the sorts of incidents that happen to those of us in the business and when they are least expected. They represent normal human snafu's that can occur with anyone. The processing of dead human beings always requires diligent and honest effort to provide dignity and professionalism in every case.

It is best if you approach your work n a mortuary as a dignified approach to serving families in their time of need. Whenever working with families, dignity is always paramount. The loss of a loved one is a very serious matter to them and many of the family members may have never had to face such a devastating event so close t them. This is a very serious time for them and they must be served in that manner.

In contrast, we recognize that people are people and it is curious how events surrounding a funeral can be humorous.

As you have probably noticed, I have included some short humorous stories after each chapter regarding some additional incidents I encountered during my work in the mortuary.

## #1  Where am I going?

We received a call from the cargo department of an airline.  They said that there had been a mixup in the paperwork for two bodies we had arranged to ship to two different cities.  It turned out that the destinations had been switched and they were on their way to the wrong cities.  The funeral director sprang into action and made several calls to the airlines and - especially to the cities where the receiving mortuaries were located.

In the end, both flights made stops at intermediate airports and the remains were realigned and sent to the proper cities.  What a way to have a disastrous result from a simple process.  I wonder how a receiving funeral director with an impending funeral service might react when he opened a casket and found the <u>wrong body</u>!

## #2  Who's Your Boyfriend?

My home was situated between the mortuary and the airport.  It was the mortuary procedure for us to use a removal van to move bodies between the mortuary and the airport and also to the Medical Examiner's Office.  Bodies to be shipped had to be taken to the cargo section of particular airlines.  This was a familiar job for me since I was still training to do embalming and trainers were sometimes too busy to work with me.  On these trips, it was my habit to stop for a moment at my house to greet my wife.

My next-door neighbor had begun to notice the frequent stops of a certain white delivery van.  At one point, he was in the yard when I drove up; as I left, he inquired of my wife and teasingly asked her asked if she had been going to the curb to meet with a boyfriend who drove by frequently in a white van and that he had noticed that she would share a little kiss with him.

When she heard that, she laughed and said, "That is no boyfriend, that is my husband who is transporting bodies to and from the airport in his part-time job at the mortuary." The laugh was on him.

## #3  The Power of Words

My wife was always reluctant to believe that I was actually involved in a mortuary. She would not even allow me to drive in front of it while she was in the car. As with many people, she always had an eerie feeling about such matters.

A few weeks after I began working a the mortuary, the boss decided to have a party for the staff. His home was next door to the mortuary and his wife could readily move about between the two buildings, so, when he proposed to have a staff party, I I automatically assumed that it would be next door - at his home.

In my eagerness to announce the party to my wife, I carelessly said to her, "Hon, we're having a Bar-Be-Cue at the mortuary tomorrow night - would you like to go?" She jumped back about ten feet and, with a shriek, and said, "Are you kidding?" She had visions of a gory event which would confirm the thoughts she had always had about shenanigans happening in mortuaries. She had read about the Asian who had a mortuary next to his brother's restaurant and evil trades were happening between them. The was the first time I had told her that the mortician (owner) where I worked actually lived next door and that the party would be his house.

## #4  Sunstroke? . . . or not

After some training, the day finally arrived when I could begin to do an unobserved embalming (no supervision). I was very ready and confident that I could do it errorlessly, after all, it was a case that required no "special" effort or considerations. It was merely a straight forward embalming case. I completed the shaving and closed the mouth and eyes set the face and creamed it generously. I began to fill my pump with formalin, water and dye.

Formalin is a clear aqueous solution of formaldehyde (which has a small amount of methanol). I then added my dye to it (as sort of reddish-brown color). When I added it to the mix, for a second, I had forgotten how much to use, so, I used the entire bottle. It seemed as if the mixture was darker than when I had watched the other people do the embalming. (first clue).

I set the hoses and the pressure and inserted the cannula in the descending carotid artery so as to embalm the body first (head last). I activated the pump and began to massage the fingers and watched as the skin began to change color (without the dye, the skin would be completely pale). I switched to the head and, reduced the machine pressure and completed the head. To my horror, the face had and body become very brown as if he had been left in the sun for over a day! I panicked and tried to empty the tank and start over with a clear liquid. About that time, my supervisor came in to see if I was finished. When he looked at my results, he laughed - until I told him that I had wasted a half tank of embalming fluid in an attempt to correct my error - TOO MUCH DYE!

## #5 Flower display - everywhere!

In every case, you wonder what kinds of things could go wrong. Every precaution is taken to avert a problem. In the end, some problems happen inside and others outside.

On this particular day, we were preparing for a very large funeral. The flowers kept pouring in and I was charged with arranging the flowers on the stage highlighted by a large lattice-work trellis which was to be used to hang many flower bouquets. I was making good progress and I still had a half hour before the guests were scheduled to arrive. I had a little difficulty placing flowers on the highest point of the trellis. I used a small stool to assist me to reach the peak. I was nearly finished when the trellis gave way and fell on me and I tumbled with it to the floor. There I was, covered with flowers and potting soil and the trellis lying on top of me. At that point, a half hour was not enough time to clean up the mess. My fall was heard in the office, so, everyone charged in to help me to complete the cleanup and a renewed effort to start over again in time for the funeral

## #6  Hold on a minute!

It was a warm and clear day as we prepared for the funeral.  I was sent ahead with the flower car to the cemetery.  I was told to gather a couple of containers and fill them with dirt from the grave.  I completed that task as the funeral procession arrived.  The funeral director asked me to stand at the end of the grave where people could walk by and take from dirt from the bowls and sprinkle it into the grave over the casket after the eulogy.

The containers I had selected were large cemetery bowls and I had to hold them during the entire interment service - I was certain that the eulogy would never end.  It was very warm in my 3-piece suit, my arms were straining to hold these two heavy vessels and I was beginning to sweat visibly.  My nose began to itch and the sweat was streaming down my face.

Finally the prayers and dedication were finished and the people began their walk around the grave; they passed by me, one by one to get their handful of dirt to sprinkle.  I think they must have felt sorry for me as I stood there sweating and twitching and I was feeling the onset of rigor mortis in my arms.

When I arrived home, I was again met with the hose in the yard.  My wife asked me if I was aware that the temperature outside had reached 106 degrees!!!  I said, "Gee, I thought it was 130 degrees!"

## #7  Timber!

It was a normal day as I previewed the day's work ahead.  I saw a body on a cot with a sheet over it with half his legs and feet exposed and extending well beyond the end of the cot.  He was over 7 feet tall.  I thought that this will require more than two of us to move him to the embalming table.  I was thinking that we would have to place an order for a specialty (oversized) casket. I was then told that he had no next of kin and that it would be sent to the county for a pauper's burial. We would be preparing him by doing a basic light embalming on him and that we would use a basic wooden container for him.

When it was time to embalm the tall man, my partner and I were alone and we proceeded to move this 'giant' from the cot to the table. We rolled him up to the embalming table - he was much longer and, I thought it would be difficult to control the draining once he was on the table once we had begun the process. We didn't have a chance to find out because as we attempted to hoist him onto the table, the end of the cot rose up there was a loud thud as he slid off the cot which had tipped; **he hit the floor!** He was very top-heavy and the two of us could not get him back up on the table (nor the cot) - we flattened the cot to the floor and wrestled him up on it. We left him in lying in the corner of the room with a sheet over him and waited until some of the other staff members returned to help us lift him onto the embalming table. Of course,, we had difficulty controlling the draining and we had a massive cleanup to do after we were finished with that case.

### #8  Don't forget your boots . . .

A lady from Texas was making arrangements for her husband. It was meant to have him go as a "True Texan." She said that she had brought his apparel for him to wear at his funeral. She then produced a nice sequin-emblazoned western-style suit, a bolo tie, a large cowboy-style hat (at least 10 gallon), a carved leather belt with a huge buckle and finally a beautiful pair of cowboy boots. We agreed to make certain that these would be used as requested.

We completed his preparation and loaded him in the casket - all except for his hat and his boots. The hat was too large could not be placed on his head, so we placed it near his hands. His feet had swelled and were distorted, so, we covered them with men's socks and the boots were nicely placed at his feet.

We thought that it was a very nice presentation, but, the wife was upset because she wanted the hat to be <u>on his head</u> and his boots <u>on his feet</u>. We explained the problems; the hat would not work since he was lying down on a pillow - she insisted on having his hat placed on his head. We also told her that the feet (typically) swelled and they become distorted at death, so we could not get his boots on his feet. We had tried, but it was impossible to get them his feet. She was audibly upset and left in a huff.

My director remained very calm since he was anxious to please the grieving customer. When the lady returned to see what we had done, she was amazed to see her husband in the casket and wearing his cowboy hat and the cowboy boots on his feet just as she had expected. The casket was an expensive full-couch unit with a full length lid which exposed the entire body. The final presentation was a great hit with the family members and the guests at the funeral.

I asked the director if the lady had asked how he had done it. He said, "No, and I didn't have the heart to tell that I had cut the hat in half and I had to slit the boots down the back." The front part of the hat had been cut off and was glued to his head and the back missing portion of it nested nicely into the pillow. The boots were prominent on his feet and looked naturally positioned.

This was a good example of how a funeral director can solve a problem through innovation and creativity. The use of various, sometimes, unorthodox or creative approaches to problems was well demonstrated in this situation. This situation could have had a disastrous ending to a real bad set of circumstances; the aplomb shown by the funeral director was very evident and contributed to a happy ending for everyone involved - especially the customer.

#### #9  Not so fast, buddy!

It was a clear day when I was asked to pick-up a body at the Medical Examiner's Office. Traffic was pretty busy. I loaded the body at the M.E.'s Office onto the cot and into the van, drove by my house, kissed my wife and drove off to take the body to the mortuary. At about the half-way point of the trip, I noticed that a motorcycle policeman with his red light was coming up on me from the rear. I swallowed hard and realized that he wanted me to pull over. I made a stop and tried to assure my window sign was in its proper place. The sign had a statement on it which read, "Funeral Vehicle on Official Business." The officer stopped and dismounted his motorcycle and walked slowly up the side of the van <u>with his hand on his pistol</u>. I rolled my window down and greeted him. He asked me if I was aware of the speed limit in this area. I said no and apologized. He hadn't seen my sign because in my haste, the sign slipped down into the window gap in the door.

He asked where I was going in such a hurry. I told him that I was delivering a body to the mortuary. He could tell that there was an odor emanating from the vehicle. I invited him to inspect the van if he desired.

He caught a whiff, stopped short and stepped back about three steps and said, "No, I believe you." Move on, but, watch your speed." I was glad that was over. As I prepared to continue my trip, he said one last thing - "By the way -I hope that when its my turn, **you** will be driving!"

I have also found that gas station attendants will give you priority when you tell them what you are carrying - especially if you are driving a funeral coach.

### #10 Double Service?

The funeral was going well until we arrived at the gravesite. We unloaded and gathered the pallbearers and prepared them to walk the casket to the gravesite. At about the halfway point, a person from the cemetery office came out and told us that we had been directed to the wrong gravesite.

We quickly reversed the procession and replaced the casket in the funeral coach. Everyone was redirected to another gravesite and they grumbled a bit, but, headed for their cars and drove on ahead of us. The office had dispatched a go-cart to lead us to the proper grave. We secured everything and got into the car - the car did not start. After several tries, my partner opened the hood. He didn't see anything wrong, but, apparently, the battery in the hearse had died (sic) - we couldn't move.

We decided to have the pallbearers return (with some additional help); we were able to load one end of the casket onto the go-cart the men held onto the end which extended beyond the cart and we carried the casket to the new location (about 3 blocks). I was glad we had good weather since the pooled water had drained off a couple of days earlier.

## #11 Who is in charge?

This a story about the beauty of a funeral arrangement. The idea of death and funerals is not a usual topic of discussion with most families. As a result, the family members are confronted with a need to make instant decisions at a time when they are least able to cope with it.

When a person dies, family members collect from everywhere - some from out of town - they amass to decide how to proceed with the head-on choices they have to make regarding the funeral and the disposal of the remains. Will they bury **or** cremate, or cremate **with** a burial? How much will that cost? Will there be a casket? How much will each part cost? Will there be a full service or just a memorial service? Is there need for a cemetery plot? How much will that cost? What about a grave marker? How much will that cost? If cremated, how shall we divide the ashes? How is it to be paid and who will pay it? The questions are never-ending. There have been huge family arguments which have taken place during the meeting to arrange a funeral.

In one situation, a large family had lost their matriarch and several members of the family came to help plan the funeral, et al. When they were taken into the showroom, a huge argument broke out. I heard things, such as: "Mom would not have want to spend that much!" and, "Mom deserved the best!" They postponed making a choice. They then argued about a cremation and an urn, they agued about the cemetery costs. It was three meetings before it all settled down.  Once again it was the calm direct guidance of the Funeral Director which made it all came together.

It goes to show that it is smart to make **prearrangements** prior to a death. The ensuing burden of the family can be avoided.

### #12  Panic in the prep-room!

One day, a body was delivered to us on a cot.  When we removed the cover sheets, we found that the body was wrapped in a bright yellow plastic sheet which had nuclear radiations symbols all over it.  The main thing, however, was that in addition to the warning labels, one could hear a semi-shrill, but muffled, murmuring tone emanating from the body.  We all began to panic (we are always concerned with contact with disease).  What about radiation?  We wondered if we are all going to be irradiated!  We placed it in a body storage cooler and refused to touch it until we knew more about it.

The boss began calling everyone - the police, the government and anyone associated with nuclear accidents. He locked the doors and sent all the administrative staff home.  He offered the staff the option of going or staying - myself and a couple of others opted to stay.

Representatives of all the agencies he had called arrived and everybody smocked up in dangerous disease uniforms - we all looked like moon-landers.

Arriving agents from the Nuclear Safety Office dressed in their special protective suits and grabbed their Geiger counters.  They scanned the body.  There were no radioactive readings so they decided to unwrap the several layers from around the body.  When that was completed, they scanned it again - the results, again, were negative, but, we could still hear that tone.  When it all seemed clear, they unwrapped the body and rolled it over.  We all cowered in the corner awaiting the discovery of something of a sinister nature.

They carefully probed and then discovered a device  which had been imbedded in his back.  When they removed it with a medical instrument, it was freed and the tone became louder.

Finally, after all the eerie apprehension, the mystery was solved - they found that IT WAS THE MAN'S HEARING AID which had been left in the "on" position and turned up!!  When he died, the hospital staff had placed him on the cot not knowing that his hearing aid was there on the cot and it had imbedded itself into the man's back.

## #13  A fly in the Ointment

It was a large funeral wake; every seat was filled.  This was set up as a public viewing on the evening before the funeral service which was to be held on the following day.

The case involved a gentleman who had died from head injuries as a the result of a motorcycle accident.  He had incurred severe injuries to his face.  We had originally suggested that the casket remain fully closed, but the family insisted on having a viewing.  His restoration job required a great amount of time and plenty of wax and makeup.

We completed the reconstruction of his face and prepared him for a viewing.  On the evening of the viewing, I was greeting arrivals at the door; about one half hour into the session, a gentleman came up to me and said that he was the brother of the deceased.  He had been sitting in the front row and he noticed that a pesky fly was hanging around the deceased in the casket.  I was immediately moved to go forward to check this out.  I stepped up to the casket and pretended to adjust the coat and tie and I swished the fly away.  (We had not provided a casket veil).  I returned to my station at the door and it was not long before the brother of the deceased approached me again to tell me about the fly.  I retraced my steps and tried to usher the fly out the side door.  I returned to my station and, again, the man approached me to report the same thing again.  I went into the office and grabbed a flyswatter and handed it to him.  (We had plenty of fly swatters on hand and always made certain that one did not get into the prep room).

As I continued my greetings a the door, it was only about 2 minutes until heard a loud "SMACK" coming from the viewing room. When I approached the casket this time, the brother was standing there with a sheepish grin with the flyswatter in his hand. When I saw the body, I beheld the strangest scene ever. There in the middle of the corpse's forehead was a dead fly and the wax and makeup had been smashed and had left a waffle-like pattern which had been imbedded by the fly swatter!

At that point, of course, we had to remove the casket from the room to redo the makeup. We told the visitors that a fly had entered the room so we armed several people with flyswatters and took the body to the prep room for repairs. After that was completed, we returned the casket to the chapel room and hoped that no further events with flies would occur.

## #14 Speaking of Flies . . .

I was vacuuming the chapel, in preparation for a funeral. The body was there, in the casket. Everything was in place; the flowers were all arranged, the music was on and we were ready.

I took a look at the body in the casket as I had intended to make a last inspection to be certain that the clothing was set properly. I was very surprised when I looked at the body and saw that the the upper lip was moving. I jumped back and checked again - it, in fact, was moving. I ran to the office and told the boss; he ran out to the chapel (it was almost time for the family to arrive).

He took a close look and saw that, in fact, the lips were moving. We quickly unlocked the bier and rolled the casket into the prep room. He grabbed a couple of instruments and opened the mouth and he revealed that a small nest of maggots had taken up residence under the man's lip and their crawling movements under the lips gave the strange appearance that I had seen. I was relieved that the family had not seen those "loose lips." After cleaning out the area and a resetting of the mouth and lips a good amount of super-glue was used to insure that the mouth was sealed.

## #15  Loose Wheels

This is the story about that uncooperative cot that every one in the mortuary business has experienced.  It was the first time I could get my wife to go to the Mortuary with me.  It took great effort to get her to agree to visit my new workplace.  When we arrived, I could feel her fearful anticipation as to what she might see.  I knew she was afraid, but, I also knew that she was curious.  She met the owner and the crew.  While were standing in the driveway between the mortuary and the owner's home, the owner's wife drove up in a van  She had just returned from a body pick-up in another town and transported him to this her mortuary.

She greeted all of us and I introduced my wife to her.  My wife was a little astonished that a woman would want to drive a van carrying a body in between cities.  She replied, "It's not bad, besides, I don't worry about someone changing the radio station or eating my potato chips.  My wife told her that she had been apprehensive about coming to visit, but that she was now more at ease now and appreciated the fact that a woman could work in this environment.

At that moment one of the men was taking the cot out of the van.  The first of the wheels came down nicely ands locked into place and he rested them on the ground.  My wife was tense and she squeezed my arm very tightly.  He gently pulled the cot farther out and when the end of it was almost out the second pair of wheels dropped into position but did not lock into place, so they buckled and the rear of the cot (with the deceased man on it) fell to the ground with a great thud!  At that point, my wife (grabbed my arm) shrieked and jumped back and (I think) nearly cut off my circulation!  I tried to assure her that this was a very rare thing that she had witnessed.  She urged me to leave and cancel the rest of the tour of the facility I had had in mind.  On the way home, I assured her that the owner would either repair the cot or replace it.

## #16  Where Did She Go?

On another occasion, I convinced my wife to go with me one evening

to a hospital to remove a body.  I told her that she would not have to
do anything - just observe.  To my surprise, she agreed.  It was a stormy
night (with lightning and everything).  We drove to the mortuary to get
a van and the paperwork associated with the case.  The rain increased
as we approached the hospital - and, by now, - it was fully dark, except
for the flashes of lightning which lit the streets.  We entered the security
gate, signed it and drove to the rear of the hospital and found a narrow
ramp which led to the basement.  It was so narrow that I had to pull both
of the outside mirrors of the van inward all the way.  I became severely
drenched in that process.  We reached the bottom of the ramp and it then
occurred to me that we would have to go back up that ramp in reverse!
Apparently, we had entered through a an exit ramp.

After unloading the cot, we entered the hospital and found the morgue.
A nice attendant greeted us in the office and he checked the paperwork
before he released the body.

He led us to the 'cooler,' checked toe tags and identified the one I
was to take.  He was then called to answer the telephone and I was
left on my own to transfer the body from his gurney to my cot.  I
started to do it, but, the wheels on the gurney began to roll and the
attempt to transfer he body was unstable; the gurney kept moving
away.  All I could do was ask my wife to place her foot next to the
wheel on the gurney grab a leg and pull.  After she had recovered
from shock she covered her face and grabbed a leg and, together,
we completed the task.  She was still in shock as we left the morgue.

The cot was loaded onto the van, closed it securely and I looked for
an exit.  I asked the morgue attendant - he told me that I had come in
the exit and all I had to do now was go our the same way I had entered.

The rain had increased and the thunder and lightning were severe. The
water was at least 3 or 4 inches deep.  Carefully (inch-by-inch) we
traveled up that ramp in reverse with little or no space or visibility
on either side.

We finally got underway to take the body to the mortuary.  My wife
refused to sit back in her chair because of our load.  I told her not to

be a "fraidy-cat." We came to a stop light and I began to stop - when the brakes caught, the cot rolled up and hit the back of our seats. My wife screamed!

When the light turned green, I accelerated the van and the cot lunged to the rear and slammed against the rear doors. She screamed again! I wondered whether the body might exit the rear doors. I stopped and went to the rear of the van, checked the floor locks and found that they were broken and could not hold the cot properly. We completed the trip with several front and rear bumps. I reported the problem, to the boss and he promised to have it replaced before it would go out again.

Needless to say, my wife was glad that trip was over and she was not anxious to repeat a trip like that. She also warned me to have that cot repaired before I leave a body on the street. I had heard of stories like that but, I certainly didn't want it to happen to me.

I believe that, to this day, she hasn't forgiven me about that one.

### #17  Where are we going - funny . . . . . . . . . . or not?

It was a hot summer day and I was tasked with taking a body to another State. My wife agreed, reluctantly, to go along since it would be several hours before I would return. She preferred to take the trip over staying home alone.

The trip started out nicely until about 150 miles out of town. We were in the hot desert approaching afternoon and I felt a bump and realized that we had blown a tire! I struggle to hold the road and pulled off into a deserted area (except for some cactus plants). I exited the car and sure enough, a rear tire had blown and I had my wife and a dead body with me stranded in "nowhere." A few cars had passed, but they didn't want to deal with a hearse (I guess). My wife and I tried to come up with some strategies.

If I continued on my own, she would be left alone in the dessert with a dead body. If we both went on, we would have to leave an unattended dead body in the desert - that's illegal. It seemed like a no-win situation.

Finally, a large Bonneville convertible slowed down and the driver offered assistance. When I approached the car, I found it full of hippie-type individuals. I was hesitant, but, I told them of my plight and they offered to help me change the flat tire.

Well,. . . I had no spare tire, so, they helped me to jack the car up and remove the wheel. That was very difficult because we had a heavy casket in the car and the sand under the jack was very loose and would not hold the car up for an extended period. The car finally settled into the sand as the jack sunk into it. I was fortunate that we had been able to remove the tire. After it was removed, these people offered to take us to the next town.

It is illegal to leave a body unattended anywhere. The only solution was to accept the offer for myself. I would ride with them and take the tire to the next town. Unfortunately, that meant that my wife was to be left behind to STAY IN THE STRANDED HEARSE - IN THE DESERT - WITH A DEAD BODY! I used my mobile telephone to call our mortuary for help so she could get home safely. I told them that the hearse was disabled and my wife was staying with the car until they could come to get the hearse (and the body) and have the coach towed. I asked them to take my wife her either to the mortuary or to her home.

After that, I gave her a goodbye kiss with the promise that I would return soon. She gave me a tearful good bye. I loaded the tire and myself into the Bonneville; I squeezed into the middle of the rear seat with the tire braced between my knees. The top was down; of course, it had no air conditioning. (I don't think either worked). The music was very loud. I was wearing a suit and tie and began to sweat profusely. We drove for about two hours and finally entered a small town and began to look for a gas station. We passed one which was closed; we finally had to ask someone where to find one. He directed us to a place 5 blocks away. It was open, so, we drove in and unloaded the tire; I thanked my partners (sic) and said goodbye. They said they wanted to stay to make certain that I was able to get the tire fixed. I declined and thanked them, gave them a tip and said goodbye. I took the tire into the garage.

I waited a short time was then told that the tire had ripped and could not be repaired and that I needed a new tire. I said OK, but, after he had searched his stock, he returned to tell me that he didn't have the right sized tire. He said he could get one and have it sent to his store. I said OK and sat at his store for at least an hour. It was getting late, but, the tire finally arrived. The tire was mounted and I paid him left with my thanks and said goodbye. I asked the tire man how I could get a ride back to my car. He didn't offer any suggestions; this meant another hitch hike the other way. He paused and said, " Wait, I know a sheriff here and I bet he could take you." He called the sheriff and he agreed to take me back to my car. He was also able to radio to the sheriff of my town to report my situation. The sheriff in my town notified the mortuary. What luck!

The sun was barely peeking over the horizon when we set out. It was sometime later when we arrived back at the area where I had broken down. The hearse had been driven back to the mortuary. It was easy to spot the area since it was dark and about five other sheriffs cars and a tow truck had stopped there with flashing red and blue lights.

As I left the Sheriff's car, I noticed that one of our mortuary workers was there to monitor the tow truck. He and another staff member has been sent to the location: one had taken my wife (and the body) back to the mortuary. The hearse was now on the tow truck's hook as the Sheriffs observed and they told me that my wife was OK.

I called to tell her that I was on the way back. The the truck drove away and I thanked every one then drove back to the mortuary. When I finally saw my wife, I could tell that she was furious with me. I was reminded that she was the reluctant one regarding this business; she was the one who would not even drive by the mortuary at first.

In the end, this was not really a funny story (except for the ride with the hippies) and I know that my wife will need a couple of decades to forgive me for this one - - - - - - - - - again.

These stories illustrate how someone could find the job in a mortuary interesting. Every day brings surprises. The maintenance of a caring and friendly demeanor is important in this business yet, on any given day, you are sure to experience things not usually found in other workplaces.

The mortuary is not something to be feared. It is superstition and ghost stories that have given them a name that strikes fear into a lot of people. Mortuaries are simply beautiful homes and they seek to offer a comfortable setting with friendly professionals who work for families who gather there to grieve and to plan. There have been stories about unethical morticians such as the 2002 Tri-State case of the abandoned bodies. Such cases are rare since rules regarding the establishment and operation monitor mortuaries throughout the United States. Mortuaries are under great scrutiny to assure that public health is protected and that professionalism and integrity are prominent; the incidences of malpractice are few and far between all around the country. Morticians are business people, but they are also people who care about families and the want to assure that loved ones are treated properly and professionally.

## Epilogue

This has been a trip into the world of thanatology, the purpose of which was to inform the curious as to the processes and procedures that are entailed in care for the dead. We always are aware that these deceased are *human beings* and that they all have families (somewhere). It reminds us of the care and dignity we must offer in a service profession that requires unique interests and skills.

We must also remember that the body is a container into which our humanness resides. That humanness derives from a God-given soul which has allowed us to experience a physical life. More importantly, we must also be concerned with the spiritual aspect of our being so that when we depart this life, we realize that an afterlife will greet us. The question is, have we prepared ourselves for entry into heaven, or, will we be remanded to the depths of Hell? Our approach and understanding of death is ameliorated by some understanding of the spiritual life. We must not ignore the fact that God has created us in his image; we must appreciate all aspects of that which make us human and be ready for what He has planned ahead for us. Remember John 14:2 "I my Father's house there are many mansions . . . I go there to prepare a place for you."

We must be careful that we don't place too much of our understanding of life to that which represents our physical being. If we wrap ourselves up in all that is physically us, we will miss the great calling that will provide an everlasting afterlife.

All the traditions and physical gaudery of the funeral cannot be appreciated by ourselves as we will be occupied with our own direction after life. It is our survivors who will look at our remains and internalize their own mortality. Our demise might serve as a way to remind our loved ones who are left behind that there is more to life than that which is represented by our physical being. The mortician attempts to create a wonderful memory picture of the deceased so that the survivors and have a pleasant vision of us as they say good-bye.

There is always the dilemma as to what part of the life of the deceased they want the mortician to show. Did the family prefer him/her to look ages younger or more like the last time they saw him/her? Many times, they will bring in a photograph of the deceased; they are usually photographs of the person in their youth - look at the obituary notices in the newspaper. Another question had to do with the consideration of his/her last appearance. Did he/she look too ill to present him/her with that presence?  There are times when you wish you could be a magician - this is one of those times.

We can bury our bodies, but we cannot bury our spiritual being, but there are professionals who can care for our physical bodies (carcasses) which are returned to the earth.  If our spiritual preparation is sound, we need not worry about the disposal of our bodies - for we will be restored with new bodies at the rapture. Psalm 23 reminds us about this: "Surely goodness and kindness shall follow me all the days of my life; and I will dwell in the house of the Lord forever."

For those who still ponder their fate, I recommend Harry Otsuji's eBook entitled, "Where Are You Going?"  It provides a guideline for the ultimate question and how to attain salvation.  It acknowledges that our ultimate hope is in Jesus Christ.

I am reminded of the scripture from John 3:16 -

> "*For God so loved the world that he gave his only begotten son, that whosoever believeth in Him should not perish but have everlasting life.*"

. . . and from 1 Corinthians 15:16 -

> "*O death, where is thy sting, O grave, where is thy victory?*"

This book has attempted to inform you of most of the aspects regarding the disposal of human remains.  It is the story of one man's exposure to it.  It tells the story of a very young man and how he was first exposed to the funeral business of body disposal.  It follows his travels through the various aspects of the death experience and provides eye-opening visions of the various processes which typically occur behind closed doors.

We have had Morticians around for a long time and their skills and their desire to care for surviving family's when they have lost a loved one.  Their skills are vital to the resolution of a death and are an invaluable component of the service industry Once a hand-me-down business, it has become a highly-trained profession.

Over eons of time, man has tried to understand life and how to avoid death.  Death has mocked man's efforts use science to extend life, however, we must eventually face it.  Since we can't avoid it, we need to learn how to deal with it.

Welcome to the world of THANATOLOGY!!

# Glossary of Funeral-related Terms

**AFTERLIFE** - An expected existence after one has died.

**ALGOR MORTIS** - The cooling off of the body immediately after death to room temperature and temporary stiffening of the muscles.

**APPRENTICE** - The name generally applied to an individual licensed to learn the embalming and funeral directing procedures under the supervision of a licensed embalmer.

**ARRANGEMENT ROOM** - A room of the funeral home used to make the necessary funeral arrangements with the family of the deceased.

**ASPIRATE** - The process of drawing fluids and gases from the abdominal cavity.

**BEREAVED** - The immediate family of the deceased; or, suffering from grief upon the death of a loved one.

**BIER** - A folding moveable stand (with lockable wheels) which is used to move caskets and can be used to hold a casket during funeral services or used transport a casket. (See Church Truck).

**BRAIN DEATH** - the final cessation of activity in the central nervous system as indicated by a flat electroencephalogram for a medically predetermined length of time.

**BURIAL** - The placing of a dead body in an underground grave or an above-ground chamber into a grave.

**BURIAL CERTIFICATE OR PERMIT** - A legal paper issued by the local government authorizing the burial. The permit may authorize earth burial or cremation or removal to a distant point.

**BURIAL GARMENTS** - Wearing apparel that has been especially designed for the dead.

**BURIAL INSURANCE** - An insurance policy wherein the principal is paid for a funeral service and/or merchandise rather than cash.

**BURIAL VAULT** - A boxlike container for covering a casket for earth burial which prevents the collapse of the grave after burial.

**CANNULA** - A small metal tube used to connect a hose with another liquid-pumping device.

**CANOPY** - A roof-like structure which allows family and/or visitors to board and alight from vehicles to protect them from the elements; a portable canvas shelter used to cover the gravesite to protect family and visitors.

**CARRIAGE** - A historical term for the predecessor of the hearse (funeral coach)

**CASKET** - A receptacle of wood or metal into which the dead body is placed for burial. It is also referred to as a "coffin: or "burial case."

**CASKETING** - Placement of the body into a casket after embalming, dressing and cometizing.

**CASKET RACK** - A device which allows caskets to be placed one atop another for display purposes; it may contain several shelves.

**CASKET VEIL** - A silk or transparent drape over the open area of a casket. Its purpose is to keep flies and other insects away from the remains.

**CATAFALQUE** - A stand upon which the casketed remains at rest while instate and during a funeral service. (See also BIER). It is more formal than a bier.

**CEMETERY** - An area of ground set aside for burial or entombment which may be publicly or privately owned.

**CENOTAPH** - An empty tomb or monument erected in memory of a person buried elsewhere.

**CERTIFIED DEATH CERTIFICATE -** (See Death Certificate).

**CHAPEL -** A large room of the funeral home in which a farewell service is held. It is primarily used for religious services; it is a room that is required for the opening of a funeral home.

**CHURCH TRUCK -** A collapsible bier.

**COFFIN -** A wedge-shaped burial case (usually 8-sided) and narrow at the3 bottom. ("Toe-pincher.").

**COLUMBARIUM -** A structure of vaults lined with recesses for urns containing cremains.

**COMMITTAL SERVICE -** The final portion of the funeral service at which time the deceased is interred or entombed.

**CONTAINER -** A pressboard or fiber box the size of a casket usually used for immediate/direct cremations; can also be used to refer to the burial urn.

**CORONER -** A public official and in some cases, a constitutional officer whose duty is to investigate the case of death if it appears to be from natural causes, or if there was no attending physician for a long period of time prior to the death. He may serve without a medical degree.

**CORTEGE -** The funeral procession.

**COSMETIZING -** The act of applying cosmetics. (See also FARDING)

**COSMETOLOGY -** Utilization of cosmetics to restore a lifelike appearance to the deceased.

**CREMAINS -** The remains of a body after cremation; a word made from "cremated-remains."

**CREMATION -** A process which reduces the body, by heat, into small bone fragments. The fragments are pulverized and reduced to the consistency of coarse sand or crushed seashells.

**CREMATORY -** A building with a furnace called a retor, t which is used to cremate human remains. (Also used to refer to the retort itself).

**CRYPT -** A vault or a room used for keeping remains.

**COT -** A stretcher-like carrier used to remove deceased persons from the place of death to the funeral home.

**DEATH -** Permanent cessation of all vital functions without the possibility of resuscitation. It is the end of life.

**DEATH CERTIFICATE -** A legal paper signed by a physician that records the cause of death and lists other vital statistics data pertaining to the deceased.

**DEATH NOTICE -** The paragraph posted in the classified portion of the newspaper which publicizes the death of a person and provides details regarding the funeral service and the survivors. (Names listed are those of the immediate survivors).

**DECEASED -** A person in whom all physical life has passed.

**DIRECT BURIAL -** The body is transferred from the place of death or the funeral home in a casket or container and delivered directly to the burial site. There is no public viewing or graveside service.

**DIRECT CREMATION** - The same procedure as for Direct Burial except that the body is delivered to a crematory.

**DISINTER** - To recover a body from a grave for reburial or for further investigation.

**DISPLAY ROOM** - A room in the funeral home in which caskets, urns, burial garments and vault samples are displayed. Also called a showroom.

**DISPOSITION** - The method or final act of determining the final resting place for the deceased. There are many methods to dispose (See Chap 4)

**EMBALM (ing, ings,)** - The process of sanitizing, disinfecting and temporarily preserving a dead body by means of circulating preservative and antiseptic through the arteries and veins.

**EMBALMER** - The trained or apprentice person who embalms.

**EMBALMING FLUID** - Liquid antiseptic and preservative chemicals used in the embalming process. Formaldehyde.

**EMBALMING TABLE** - A drainable operating table constructed of metal (Stainless Steel) upon which the remains are placed for embalming.

**ENTOMBMENT** - The placement of a body in a casket in an above ground mausoleum.

**ETHICS** - The moral code which guides the members of their profession in proper conduct of their duties and obligations.

**EXHUME** - To retrieve buried remains to reexamine a body or to transfer it to another grave in the same area or in a distant cemetery.

**FAMILY CAR** - The limousine used in a funeral to transport the family of the deceased to and from the place of burial.

**FAMILY ROOM** - A special room in the funeral home which affords the family of the deceased comfort and privacy during the period of the funeral.

**FARD** - to paint a face with cosmetics.

**FARDING** - the act of cosmetizing.

**FLOWER CAR** - A vehicle used to transport flower pieces from the funeral home to the church and to the cemetery.

**FINAL RITES** - The funeral service.

**FIRST CALL** - The initial visit by the funeral home representative to the place of death for the purpose of removing the deceased and to secure certain information needed to activate the post-death procedures.

**FUNERAL ARRANGEMENTS** - The activity discussed with the families regarding the details for planning the financial and service details.

**FUNERAL COACH** - A newer term for a specially designed vehicle which carries the casket (full or empty) to its destination. Primarily used during the funeral procession. (See also HEARSE)

**FUNERAL DIRECTOR** - A specially-trained professional who plans and prepares for the burial or other disposition of dead human bodies. He supervises the activities of the funeral; he maintains a funeral establishment, counsels with survivors; he also performs embalmings.

**FUNERAL HOME** - A building used for the expressed purpose of providing funerals for families. It may contain a prep-room, a chapel, a display room, an arrangements room, slumber room, specialized vehicles and a staff of embalmers and administrative personnel.

**(The) FUNERAL RULE** - (16 CFR Part 453) - A Federal Trade Commission enforced rule that makes it possible for families to select from an itemized list only those goods and services they want or need and pay only for those selections whether pre-need or at-need. It allows for comparison of mortuaries. It does not apply to third party sellers such as casket dealers, or cemeteries without an on-site funeral home.

**FUNERAL SERVICE** - The professions which deal with handling of dead human bodies; the formal activities associated with conducting the religious and final disposition of the remains.

**FUNERAL SPRAY** - A collective mass of cut flowers arranged in a unit which is placed on the casket and kept there throughout the service and later delivered to the home of the family as a floral tribute.

**GRAVE** - An excavation in the earth for the purpose of burying the deceased.

**GRAVE LINER** - A receptacle made of concrete, metal or wood in which the casket is placed as an extra precaution in protecting the remains from the elements. It is required by most cemeteries to prevent the collapse of a grave after burial. (See Vault).

**GRAVE MARKER** - A method of identifying of a particular grave. Permanent grave markers, placed the head of the grave, are usually metal or stone which show the name of the individual, date and place of birth and the date and place of death.

**GRAVESIDE SERVICES** - Formal committal services conducted at the cemetery at the site of the burial.

**HEARSE** - An older term for a vehicle used to transport the dead to a grave. (See also FUNERAL COACH)

**HONORARY PALLBEARERS** - Friends or members of a religious, social or fraternal organization who act as an escort or honor guard for the deceased. They do not carry the casket.

**HOSPICE** - An organization dedicated to the care of the terminally ill who may choose to die at home, in the hospital or elsewhere. It is typically staffed by volunteers.

**INQUEST** - An official inquiry usually held before a jury to determine the cause of death. This is usually conducted by a coroner.

**IN STATE** - The custom of availing the deceased for viewing by relatives and friends prior and after the funeral service. (Typically called "lying in state').

**INSTRUMENTS** - The varied tools required to perform the embalming.

**INTER** - To bury a dead body in the earth in a grave, in a tomb or in a mausoleum.

**INTERMENT** - The actual burial.

**INTERMENT** - The act of placing cremains into an urn.

**LEAD CAR** - The vehicle in which the funeral director and the clergyman rides. It forms at the front of the cortege and leads the procession to the church and to the cemetery.

**LICENSE** - An authorization from the State granting permission to perform duties which, without such permission, would be illegal. (Ex. Embalmer, Funeral Director, Apprentice).

**LIMOUSINE** - A long automobile designed to seat several persons behind the driver's seat.

**LIVOR MORTIS** - Hypostasis of the blood following death; a purplish red discoloration of the skin. Forensic pathologists can use it to determine the position of the body at the time of death. Blood will settle at the lowest point and indicate how the body was lying.

**LOWERING DEVICE** - a mechanism used for lowering a casket into a grave. It is placed over the open grave. It has two or more straps which support the casket over the open grave. Upon release, the straps unwind from a cylinder and slowly lower the casket into the grave. When the casket settles, the straps are rewound from one side.

**MAUSOLEUM** - a public or private building especially designed to receive entombments. It is a permanent above-ground resting place for the dead.

**MARKER** - A monument or memorial to mark a place of burial. (See Grave Marker)

**MEDICAL EXAMINER** - A specially trained medical doctor/pathologist who is appointed by a government entity to perform autopsies on bodies which have experienced death as a result of violence, suicide, crime and other unknown causes to determine the causes of death and the circumstances which surrounded it. He performs duties of a coroner, except he is medically qualified as a Board Certified as a Forensic Pathologist.

**MEMORIAL SERVICE** - A religious service conducted in memory of the deceased without the presence of the remains/cremains.

**MINISTER'S ROOM** - A room in the funeral home set aside for the clergyman wherein he can robe and make any last minute preparations for the funeral service,

**MORGUE** - A place to where bodies are removed which contains a walk-in cooler where bodies can be held until further processing. It may also include a windowed alcove where the body can be shown for identification purposes and non-public viewing.

**MORTICIAN** - See Funeral Director.

**MORTUARY** - See Funeral Home.

**MORTUARY SCIENCE** - The study of all aspects of funeral processing regarding chemicals, health hazards, fluid balancing, Anatomy, Physiology, dissection, forensics as well as funeral home operation. Establishes protocol for the proper preparation of dead human bodies for final disposition.

**MOURNER** - A person who attends a funeral out of affection and respect for the deceased. It may include family and non-family members.

**NICHE** - A shell-like space in a wall made for the placement of urns (or other ash container) as a final resting place for cremains.

**OBITUARY** - A brief (newspaper) notice of the death of a person which usually lists the name, the age and a biographical sketch of the.

**PALLBEARERS** - Individuals whose duty is to carry the casket during the funeral service. These are usually friends and relatives. (In some places, they may be hired). See also HONORARY PALLBEARERS.

**PLOT** - A specific area of ground in a cemetery purchased by a family or an individual which usually contains two graves.

**PREARRANGED FUNERAL** - Funeral plans and arrangements prepared in advance of a person's death.

**PREARRANGED FUNERAL TRUST** - A method by which an individual or a family can prepay their funeral costs through a Trust or through a Life Insurance Policy.

**PREPARATION ROOM** - A room in a funeral home designed and equipped for preparing the deceased for final disposition. It is restricted to licensed personnel and some others who may have to provide a special service (such as dressing) inside it. (Also called the prep- room).

**PREPARATION TABLE** - A stainless steel operating table located in the prep-room upon which a body is placed for embalming and dressing.

**PRICE LIST** - An itemized list of funeral goods and services.

**PROCESSION** - The vehicular movement of the funeral from the place where the funeral service was conducted to the church and/or cemetery. It may also include the movement of the casket in a church funeral where the mourners may follow the casket in and out of the church.

**PURGE** - A discharge from the body through any orifice, especially the mouth, nose and ears. It contains matter expunged from the stomach or intestine which was caused by ineffectual embalming, due to putrefaction.

**PUTREFACTION** - The decomposition of the body which produces a foul-smelling product.

**REGISTER** - A book made available by the funeral director for recording the names of people who have visited or attended the funereal to pay respects to the deceased. It also lists vital statistics of the deceased, name of the officiating clergyman, place of interment, time and date of the service and a list of floral tributes.

**REMAINS** - The body of the deceased.

**REPOSING ROOM** - A room of the funeral home where a body may lie in state from the time it is casketed until the time of the funeral service. (See Slumber Room)

**RESTORATIVE ART** - The process of restoring mutilated and distorted features by employing wire, plaster, wax and creams. It usually entails facial work but can also refer to work on other aspects such as the hands. It is also called derma-surgery or demisurgery.

**RETORT** - An oven chamber where bodies are cremated.

**RIGOR MORTIS** - A rigidity of the muscles which occurs after death.

**SLUMBER ROOM** - A room with a bed upon which the deceased is placed prior to casketing on the day of the funeral. The body is appropriately dressed and looks normal as it lies in state. Visitors may visit the body and pay respects.

**SURVIVOR** - The person who are outliving the deceased and remain behind - particularly the family members.

**TOMOGRAPHY** - A method of producing a 3-dimensional image of the internal structure of a human body by the observation and recording of the differences in the effects on the passages of waves of energy impinging on those structures.

**TRADE EMBALMER** - A licensed embalmer who is not employed by one specific funeral home, but offers embalming services for several firms for a salary.

**TRADITIONAL SERVICE** - A religious service with the body present usually preceded by a visitation.

**TRANSIT PERMIT** - A legal document issued by the local government authorizing removal of a body to a cemetery for interment. A separate document may be required for cremations.

**URN** - A wood, marble or wood container into which cremains are placed.

**VAULT** - The metal or fiberglass or concrete container which is placed over the casket in the grave to prevent sinking of the ground over it.

**VIGIL** - A Roman Catholic religious service held on the eve of the funeral service.

**VISITATION** - A scheduled time during which a body is present in an open or closed casket when family and friends may pay their respects. It is usually in a private room. (Also called the viewing, calling hours, family hour or a wake.

**WAKE** - A watch kept over the deceased, sometimes lasting the entire night, preceding the funeral.

Made in the USA
San Bernardino, CA
22 January 2016